CLASSIC WWI AIRCRAFT PROFILES

Other titles in the series

Classic WWI Aircraft Profiles, Volume 2
The Bristol Fighter
Albatros Fighters
Nieuport Scouts
Pfalz Scouts
Sopwith Snipe
Caproni Bombers
LFG Roland

Other aviation titles

Classic WWII Aviation series
Consolidated B-24 Liberator
De Havilland Mosquito
Messerschmitt Bf 110
Lockheed P-38 Lightning

Butcher Bird: The Focke-Wulf Fw 190

CLASSIC WWI
AIRCRAFT PROFILES

Volume One

CERBERUS

Published in 2002

PUBLISHED IN THE UNITED KINGDOM BY:

Cerberus Publishing Limited
Penn House, Leigh Woods
Bristol BS8 3PF
Telephone: ++44 117 974 7175
Facsimile: ++44 117 973 0890
e-mail: cerberusbooks@aol.com

British Library Cataloguing in Publication Data.
A catalogue record for this book is available from the British Library.

ISBN 1 84145 101 0

PRINTED AND BOUND IN ITALY

Contents

Introduction

World War One could well be considered the first 'modern' war as, apart from the de-humanising aspects of trench warfare, it introduced the tank and the aircraft, both of which came to be the dominating factors in the conduct of subsequent wars and battles.

The aircraft available, at the outbreak of World War One, were little more than 'box' kites and had been developed for sport rather than a weapon of war. When, in 1914, the various military authorities of the protagonists considered the possibilities of using aircraft it was primarily in the rôle of transportation for 'observers' to reconnôitre troop movements. Officers, who were 'gentlemen', conducted the observation while the 'driver', invariably a non-commissioned officer and trained as a mechanic, flew the aircraft on the instructions of his passenger.

At the onset of war in August 1914, it was Germany and France that had the largest number of aircraft and, in Germany's case, airships. The combined total from both the Imperial German Air Service and the Imperial Naval Air Service amounted to under 300 machines and nearly half of this total were *Taube* (Dove) aircraft originally designed by an Austrian engineer Igo Etrich in 1910. French enthusiasts had taken a keen interest in developing 'flying machines' from the earliest days of manned flight and produced many innovative features that were incorporated into the designs of aircraft throughout the world. But, even they could only muster around 160 aircraft and 15 airships at the outbreak of war.

Such was the state of the Allies' (Belgium and Russia) aircraft industry in 1914 that they had to rely, heavily, on French production, therefore much of the early aerial activity was conducted with French machines. Belgium, when they were invaded on August 4, 1914, had less than 20 aircraft and suitable only for reconnaissance purposes. The Imperial Russian Air Service had around 240 aircraft, many of which were of French design and production and to this the imperial Russian Navy could add a small quantity of floatplanes and flying boats.

The British government was also caught unawares and, in the early months of the war, had also to rely heavily on French machines. The British Imperial General Staff had no concept of modern warfare and decided that should the aeroplane have a rôle it would be for obsrvation and reconnaissance. A few years earlier, in 1913, Major Brooke-Popham of the Air Battalion, Royal Engineers, did see the possibilities of 'aerial combat' and bolted a gun, in a fixed position, to his Blériot monoplane. This 'ungentlemanly' act was soon censured by his superior officers and he was ordered to remove it. About the same time the designer and manufacturer of machine-guns, Colonel Isaac Newton Lewis, demonstrated the possibilities of using the aeroplane as an offensive weapon by fitting one of his machine-guns on a Wright biplane belonging to the U.S. Army Signal Corps. Such was the reception that he left the country in disgust and subsequently established a factory in Liège, Belgium, to manufacture his guns.

The crews of the first Royal Flying Corps aircraft to be sent to France were, therefore, required to report on the enemy's troop and artillery movements but, should they encounter any Zeppelins, they were authorised to ram them! This hazardous pastime was met with very little enthusiasm by the crews, especially as parachutes and life jackets did not form part of their kit.

Early 'scout' aircraft of the German, French and British air services had the manoeuvrability to engage in combat but their crews were usually equipped with hand-guns. These needed to be fired at point-blank range and, even then, with a huge amount of luck. It was of course the machine-gun that provided the impetus and by early 1915 the Lewis and Hotchkiss machine-guns were being fitted to the Allied aircraft, later to be joined by Vickers. German machines had the LMG Parabellum, also known as the Spandau, fitted. Although these gave some form of armament there was a limitation on their use by the pilot as they were usually fitted on the top wing - to avoid shattering the propeller - or at an upward angle. Either way it needed great skill by the pilot as he would invariably have to stand in the cockpit, holding his control column between his knees, before he could fire his gun. More accuracy was achieved by the observer as his machine-gun could be turned and pivoted thus allowing him a wider range within which to fire.

It was not until the interrupter gear, allowing the machine-gun to fire through the propeller, that 'fighter' aircraft came of age. This innovation soon allowed pilots on both sides to amass 'scores' of the aircraft they shot down, and names such as Boelcke, Immelmann, Richthofen, Guynemer, Nungesser, Ball, Mannock, Bishop and Rickenbacker were soon receiving a hero's adulation.

Classic WWI Aircraft Profiles gives a short history, in text and illustrations, of many of the aircraft flown by these heroes.

CHAPTER ONE

Fokker Fighters

The name *Fokker* was synonymous with aviation in the First World War and produced some of Germany's finest military aircraft. Development of Fokker aircraft started back in 1911, when Anthony Fokker produced the first of his many aircraft, the *Spin* (Spider). In early 1913 the German Army showed interest and Fokker started to develop the Spider for military use under a specification issued by the military authorities. Work started on a series of aircraft prototypes designated 'M' for *militarisch* (military). Throughout 1913 Fokker worked on a number of types, the M.1, M2 and the M3 which, more-or-less, conformed to the German Army specification and primarily used the 95-hp or 100-hp Mercedes six-cylinder, in-line, engine, although the variant M.3A had a 70-hp Renault engine fitted. But, until the M.4, they utilised many of the designs - and faults - of the original Spider. The M.4, still powered by the 100-

Anthony Fokker's first aeroplane the Fokker Spin *(Spider) in 1910.*

hp Mercedes engine, incorporated some radical wing, tailplane and undercarriage designs that were later to appear in the ubiquitous E.1 *Eindecker*. Towards the end of 1913 the various prototypes had incurred high costs but with very little success. The financial strain was very much in evidence and Fokker appreciated that, to continue the business, he needed a new aircraft that would provide him with lucrative military orders. In desperation he remembered a Morane-Saulnier Type H that he had the opportunity of examining earlier in the year and decided to go to Paris in the hope of purchasing a second-hand machine. He managed to acquire a damaged early model that was fitted with a 50-hp Gnôme rotary engine and set about to restore it to flying condition - this gave Fokker the opportunity of not only studying its design and manufacture but also its handling capabilities. Together with one of his long-suffering designers, Martin Kreutzer, Fokker produced working drawings that

Anthony Fokker performing a loop from low altitude in a Fokker M.5L. A Spider and an M.2 can be seen in front of the hangar.

incorporated much of the Morane's design but with additional features that could be claimed as their own.

By April 1914 the moribund Fokker factory had launched into a new

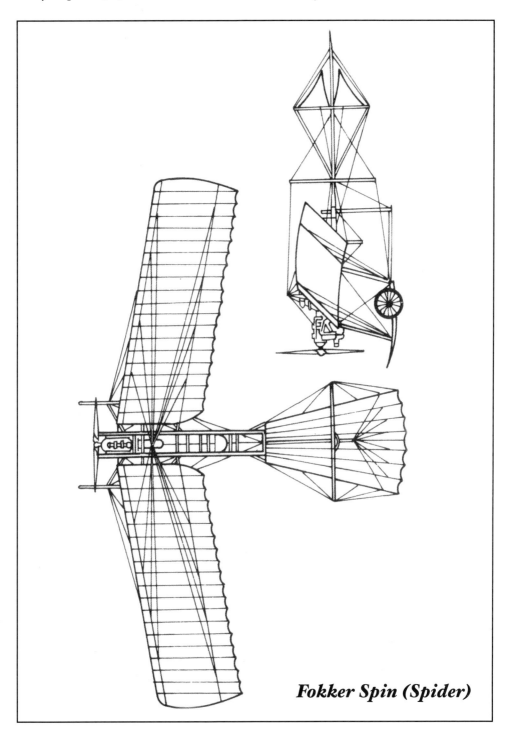

Fokker Spin (Spider)

prototype program that was designated the M.5. and consisted of two types, the M.5K and the M.5L, both powered by a 50-hp Gnôme engine. The 'K' stood for the short wingspan version, the 'L' for the long span model. However, the performance was disappointing and so a reconditioned 70-hp Gnôme engine was purchased and installed in the M.5L. The difference in performance was immediately noticeable and, together with the new comma-shaped rudder, made the aircraft an attractive proposition to the German Army. A number of both the M.5K and L models were purchased by the military and were in operation as reconnaissance aircraft when the war began. There was one further M model, the Fokker M.5K/MG on which was mounted a Parabellum machine gun for testing the synchronisation gear.

Fokker M.5K.

The synchronised gun was one of the greatest innovations of the First World War and had found its way into Fokker's hands in 1915. Up to that point there had been problems firing a machine-gun from the cockpit of an aircraft for fear of hitting and destroying the propeller. As usual with such problems, necessity became the mother of invention and this was no exception. A well known pre-war French aviator and stunt-pilot, Roland Garros, a member of *Escadrille MS23*, realised the inherent problem and designed a forward facing mounting on his own Morane-Saulnier Parasol. He had a Hotchkiss machine-gun mounted directly in front of the cockpit and wedges of armoured steel screwed to the backs of each blade to deflect any bullets fired that did not pass between them. It worked to a certain degree and, in the first part of April, he shot down and destroyed three German aircraft while using his adaptation.

French pilot Roland Garros being interrogated by German officers after being shot down. Garros attempted to destroy his aircraft with its armoured propeller that enabled him to have a fixed forward firing Hotchkiss machine-gun fitted.

On April 18, 1915, Roland Garros was attacking the railway station at Courtrai, when his aircraft was hit by a rifle bullet from the gun of a German soldier by the name of Schlenstedt. The bullet severed the Morane Parasol's fuel line and the aircraft was forced to crash land behind German lines. That bullet was to ultimately become the instrument of one of the most important influences of the art of aerial fighting during the First World War. Although Roland Garros tried to destroy his aircraft he was unsuccessful and he was captured with his aircraft intact. It did not take the Germans long to realise who they had

Roland Garros' aircraft showing the deflector plates mounted on the propeller.

captured and the prize they had in his aircraft. The wreckage of his Morane Parasol was passed to a *Hauptmann* Foerster who took it to Doeberitz, where an engineer, Simon Brunnhuber, was ordered to make a working copy of the interruptor firing mechanism. This he did and high ranking officers watched with great interest as the engine and propeller were set up on jigs and the machine-gun fired. It is not certain whether or not the steel of the deflecting plates was of armour plating or that the armour piercing bullets used were of superior quality,

Roland Garros' Morane-Saulnier showing the deflector plates fitted to the propeller blades.

but the propeller disintegrated and the whole test bed was shattered. All those watching were lucky to escape without injury. It was then decided to pass the whole project over to Anthony Fokker, who, after examining the method used to fire the machine gun and recognising its limitations, decided that instead of making copies of it he would improve on it.

A synchronised machine-gun with an interrupter mechanism had been designed by a Swiss engineer by the name of Franz Schneider who was an engineer with LVG (*Luft-Verkehrs Gesellschaft*), and patented in July 1913. When Franz Schneider was shown the drawings from Anthony Fokker's patent he questioned the originality and stated that they were based on his earlier design. Fokker maintained that Schneider's original design was based on the blocking of the machine-gun when a propeller blade was in front of the barrel. A two-bladed propeller revolved at 1200 times a minute, which meant that a blade passed in front of a gun muzzle 2400 times in a minute. Fokker's design was worked by a camshaft and lever, which fired the machine-gun the instant there was no blade in front of the gun barrel. The Parabellum gun fired 600 times in

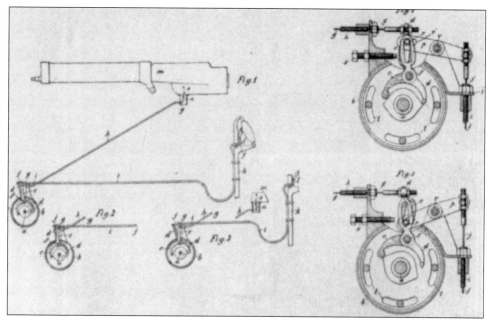

The drawing from the patent recording Fokker's invention which was hotly disputed by Swiss engineer Franz Schnieder, who claimed his idea had been stolen by Anthony Fokker

a minute, so *his* design was based on a method in which made the propeller shaft fired the gun when there was no blade in the way. In all probability the actual design was conceived by another member of Fokker's design team, Heinrich Luebbe.

Fokker and his engineers, Luebbe, Leimberger and Heber got to work and 72 hours later they had designed and built the mechanism. Every time the propeller blade lined up with the muzzle in front of the firing machine-gun, a cam, actuated by the engine, stopped the gun firing. The system was tested and fitted to a Fokker M.5K monoplane for final testing. A young *Leutnant* Oswald Boelcke was assigned to carry out the testing and after normal tests took it on a mission. After the third mission Boelcke had scored a victory (The first M.5K

A version of the interruptor mechanism set up by the Germans at Doeberitz after the capture of the Garros aircraft.

victory was by *Leutnant* Kurt Wintgens on 1 July 1915). The Germans were delighted and ordered not only the interrupter firing gear system, but also the Fokker M.5K aircraft, redesignated the E.I (*Eindecker*). With the arrival of the Fokker Eindecker and its interrupter firing mechanism, came a new threat to the Allies. By the end of the summer, the German pilots were attacking the British and French aircraft with devastating results. They had acquired air supremacy.

Fokker E.I Eindecker

The Fokker M.5K, an unarmed aircraft, was fitted with the synchronised LMG.08 machine gun and given the military designation of E.I/15 - the first of the Fokker Eindeckers. Idflieg (*Inspektion der Fliegertruppen* - Inspectorate of Aviation Troops) were so impressed with the aircraft they placed an order for fifty E.Is with Anthony Fokker but with the proviso that they build them as quickly as possible. Fokker was also ordered to go to certain airfields at the Front and demonstrate the Fokker E.I to the front line pilots. He was also to instruct the inexperienced pilots and ground crews in the handling of the aircraft and the maintenance of the guns. On one of the visits to an airfield at Stennay, Fokker gave a demonstration of the aircraft's handling qualities and air firing to the German Crown Prince. He was then ordered to go to Douai, where the air service were fighting a desperate battle over the Arras sector, and introduce the aircraft to *Leutnant* Otto Parschau. Parschau became so adept at handling the aircraft, that Fokker invited him to join him as a demonstration pilot on his visits to the airfields at the Front.

Equipped with two E.Is, Anthony Fokker and Parschau demonstrated the aircraft to a number of front line pilots, including *Leutnant* Oswald Boelcke and *Leutnant* Max Immelmann, both of whom were to use the Eindecker to great advantage and later were awarded the *Orden Pour Le Mérite*. A number of the pilots became efficient in the handling of the E.I and so the first models off the production line were sent into the Verdun and Arras areas.

There were no drawings or specifications available, in all probability there never were, such was the desperate need for aircraft at the Front. The Fokker E.I was never even given a full acceptance test by IdFlieg, so it is more than likely that the first Fokker E.Is were no more that armed M.5K/MGs. The aircraft carried enough fuel (16 gallons) and oil (3½ gallons) for two hours endurance. Because of the voracious appetite of the 80-hp Oberursel 9-cylinder rotary engine and the escort fighter duties expected of it, an additional fuel tank to the one mounted behind the engine, was mounted behind the cockpit. This gave the aircraft a flight endurance of four hours. Transferring the fuel to the

Fokker E.I Eindecker taking off.

gravity tank was carried out by means of an automatic petrol feed which was driven by a small windmill mounted on the starboard undercarriage strut.

The fuselage, as far as can be ascertained, was identical to that of the M.5K whereas the wing had a number of minor modifications. The wing spars of the E.I. were made of ash although later models had theirs made of Polish pine which was considerably more plentiful. The compression struts were made of steel tubing and fixed to the wings by means of ball-and-sockets which allowed the wings a fair degree of flexibility. The aluminium engine cowling retained the shape of that of the Morane-Saulnier, but had panels that extended further down the fuselage offering protection against the Oberursel engine's tendency to spurt flame back along the fuselage when over-primed.

The ammunition box was situated just above the pilot's knees and was made of soldered brass sheet. As can be imagined in the event of a crash landing this could cause considerable injury to the pilot's legs. One drawback to the simple design of the E.I., was that the pilot sat rather high, which although giving him a good field of vision, subjected him to the rigours of the elements.

A number of the pilots had their idiosyncrasies regarding the positioning of the guns. Some wanted them to be dead straight, whilst other wanted them mounted slightly to the starboard. To enable the pilot to draw a steady bead on their adversary, Anthony Fokker devised a tripod headrest which a number of the pilots had fitted to their aircraft.

As time progressed a number of minor modifications were made to the Fokker E.I Eindecker and new models appeared culminating in the Fokker E.IV.

Flugmeister *Boedicker in his naval uniform in fron of his Fokker E.I. Eindecker.*

Fokker E.I. Eindecker.

Max Immelmann in his Fokker E.I. flying `top cover' for a Roland C.II scout.

Max Immelmann's special Fokker E.IV with its three mounted machine-guns.

Fokker E.I Eindecker Specifications	
Description:	Single-seat fighter/scout
Wing Span:	31ft. 2 ins.
Length:	23ft. 7 ins
Height:	7ft. 10 ins.
Weight Empty:	878 lbs
Weight Loaded:	1,232 lbs
Engine:	One 100-hp Oberursel UI, rotary
Maximum Speed:	81 mph
Armament:	One fixed Spandau machine gun synchronised to fire through the propeller.

The standard Fokker E.IV being prepared for take off.

Fokker E.IV.

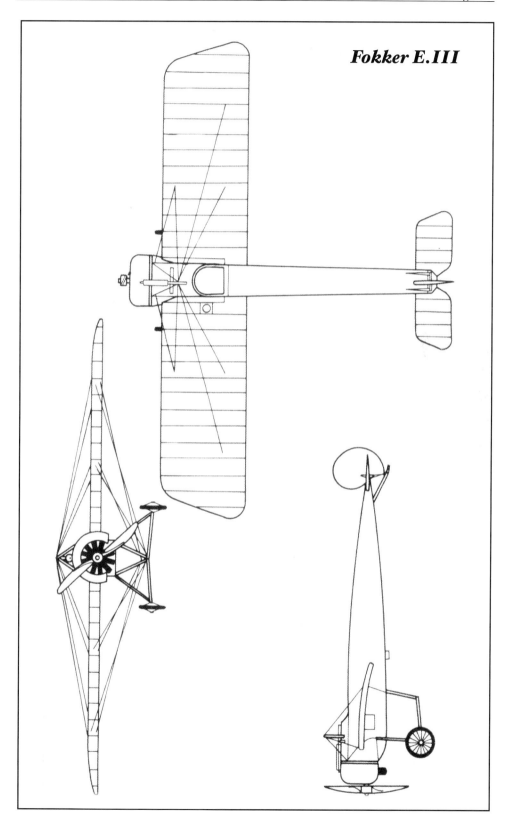

Fokker E.III

Fokker at this time was under a great deal of criticism, not only from his own countrymen but also from the Allies, about his close ties with Germany. Fokker's defence was that at the onset of the war, his aircraft had been requisitioned by the German Army, together with all the spare engines and equipment. He said that he was blamed for not placing himself at the disposal of the Allies, but argued that his own country, Holland, preferred to buy French aircraft and England and Italy never even bothered to respond to his proposals. Russia was so corrupt that it would have been impossible to deal with them and the only country who even offered to respond to him, (although it was not entirely with open arms) was Germany. It is said the British Government later even offered him a substantial sum of money to work for them.

As previously stated Fokker had developed a number of aircraft prior to the First World War, but on the day that war was declared against Britain, all German aircraft manufacturers were informed by telegram that their aviation material was under the control of the Army. Fokker was immediately inundated with requests by the German Navy and various other operational units, to buy his existing aircraft. In fact had the Allies offered to buy his aircraft, there is no doubt that Fokker would have sold them to the highest bidder. Fokker off-loaded all of his aircraft, spare parts and junk, with the exception of an M.5L *Grüner Vogel* (Green Bird) belonging to *Leutnant* von Buttlar's squadron. He also accepted orders for aircraft from the German Army and Navy as well as Austria, orders that he had no hope of fulfilling, and for this he received a severe reprimand from the Idflieg.

Fokker M.6

Fokker M.8 showing the cutaway side of the fusleage to give the pilot greater downward visibility.

The Fokker works consisted of a number of tumbledown shacks and huts, so he and his staff set to work to repair, enlarge and equip these workshops for production. The one main thing that was against Anthony Fokker, was that he was an alien in a country that was at war, and as such could expect no special entitlements.

Then Idflieg approached Fokker with the suggestion of developing a two-seat aircraft for the purposes of artillery spotting. What developed was the Fokker M.6. Based on the airframe of the M.5, the M.6 had a wingspan of 36 feet, a fuselage length of 22 feet and was powered by a 80-hp Oberursel U.O rotary engine. The aircraft completed its initial tests and was then sent to Schwerin to be evaluated by military pilots. On its second flight, the pilot, *Oberleutnant* Kolbe, with an observer by the name of *Hauptmann* Ruff got confused with the fuel cocks. The result was that the engine stopped in mid-air and the aircraft crashed whilst Kolbe was attempting to land. The aircraft was completely destroyed and the pilot Kolbe killed. The observer was lucky to escape with just minor injuries. Only one of the aircraft was ever built.

Fokker D.I.

One of the finest series of aircraft produced by Fokker, was the Fokker D, however its beginnings were hardly auspicious for when the first of the series, the Fokker D.I, was presented to the military for the first of its evaluation tests, it came in for some scathing reports. This infuriated Anthony Fokker, but unfortunately for him the reports came from two German Flying Corps officers, Professor *Dr-Ing*. Bendemann and *Dipl.-Ing*. G Madelung, who besides carrying out their normal duties were both eminent aeronautical engineers. One passage from the scathing reports read.

When seen from a distance of twenty yards the Fokker D.I makes an excellent impression. However, *Herr Direktor* Fokker is advised to imitate the technological progress embodied in the construction of the Albatros D.I, of which he has taken photographs. This suggestion relates as much to the difference in workmanship between the two aircraft as to all the technical differences of the Fokker D.I. Apart from these consideration, the wing warping needs the use of far too much force.

What became obvious very quickly, was that Anthony Fokker, whose extremely garrulous and persuasive manner had helped him in the past, was now faced with professional military aeronautical engineers who were not swayed by sales patter. They were involved in a war and wanted the finest aircraft that were available and were not prepared to put up with second best. They also issued Fokker with a severe warning about his activities when visiting the *Prüfanstalt und Weft* at Aldershof as he was seen, while there, photographing other manufacturers prototypes and experimental models They made it clear that had it been anyone else they may have found themselves facing espionage charges, pointing out the fact that Fokker would do well to remember that he was a foreigner in a country that was at war.

Notwithstanding these difficulties a number of recommendations were made and after all had been implemented, three of the aircraft were ordered. After

Martin Kreutzer standing in front of the Fokker D.I in which he lost his life on 27 June 1916 whilst testing the aircraft.

further evaluation by the air force, an additional order for twenty-five Fokker D.Is with the 120-hp Mercedes engine was made. It has to be said that during the second of the evaluation tests, the lack of any stiff opposition enabled the D.I to give a good account of itself. Some minor modifications were made and a further eighty were delivered.

Anthony Fokker claimed that his D.I aircraft was the most efficient and fastest fighter anywhere in the world, but none of the official reports substantiated this claim. On the contrary the reports claimed that the Fokker E.IV, which the D.I was destined to replace, was by all accounts far superior.

Problems arose when the aircraft was assigned to various *Jastas* on the Western Front and came up against some of the Allied aircraft, like the rotary engined Nieuport, which could outclimb, outmanoeuvre and outshoot the D.I. It wasn't long before the German pilots started to complain bitterly about the aircraft and the authorities re-assigned it to the Eastern Front on non-combat duties.

The D.I was of the conventional construction, being an orthodox two-bay biplane. The fuselage consisted of welded steel tubes the same as the 'E'model monoplane. It was braced with stranded wire cables that formed a rigid box-girder design that was covered on a doped fabric. Powered by a six-cylinder in-line, water-cooled 120-hp Mercedes DII engine, which was contained in the nose of the aircraft covered in metal panels. The radiator boxes were of the 'honey-combed' variety and were mounted adjacent to the leading edge of the wings on either side of the fuselage.

The upper and lower wings were identical in length and were of the straightforward parallel-chord layout, the upper wing being sited close to the fuselage mounted on short steel-tube struts, which in turn were welded directly onto the longerons. The wings were supported with circular steel tubes in which the warp control wires passed. The wingspan was 29ft. 8in. The D.I was initially armed with a single LMG.08/15 synchronised machine-gun but later models incorporated the twin Spandau.

The Austro-Hungarian Air Force purchased a number of D.Is from Fokker, but then the *Ungarische allgemeine Maschinefabrik AG* (MAG) of Budapest started to build the Fokker D.I under licence. A number of the aircraft were also used in Turkey and Mesopotamia.

The Idflieg ordered that eighty of the Fokker D.Is be delivered to the Western Front, but within a matter of weeks the German pilots were requesting they be replaced with either the modified Halberstadt or the Albatros D.I.

Tragedy struck the Fokker factory on 27 June 1916, when chief designer Martin Kreutzer took a Fokker D.I on an acceptance flight. Shortly after taking off the aircraft crashed and Kreutzer was dragged from the wreckage. Barely conscious the mortally injured Kreutzer managed to explain to his rescuers that a jammed rudder had caused the crash, but that didn't stop Anthony Fokker turning up and verbally berated the dying man.

Fokker D.I Specifications	
Description:	Single-seat fighter/scout
Wing Span:	29ft. 8ins.
Length:	21ft.
Height:	8ft 4ins.
Weight Empty:	844lbs
Weight Loaded:	1,267lbs
Engine:	One 120-hp Mercedes D.II, six-cylinder, in-line, water-cooled
Maximum Speed:	93mph
Armament:	One fixed Spandau machine gun synchronised to fire through the propeller

Fokker D.II.

Kreutzer's place was taken by Reinhold Platz who was instrumental in designing and producing the Fokker D.II. Although numerically the D.II should have followed the D.I, it was in fact produced earlier and evolved directly from the M.17z prototype. The D.II's welded steel tube airframe was slightly longer than that of the D.I although marginally thinner. This consequently made the aircraft lighter, and together with the nine-cylinder 100-hp Oberursel U.I rotary engine, made the D.II more manoeuvrable. The wings were also slightly smaller although the structural layout was the same.

The undercarriage was a little forward of the lower wing leading edge, giving the aircraft a rakish look. Each 'vee' was made up of three steel tubes, two of them forward and the third back. The axle was fixed between the two forward tubes, allowing it to move upwards when under tension on the elastic cord shock absorbers.

One variation of the D.II was the fitting of a fourteen-cylinder, two-row 160-hp Oberursel U.III rotary engine after the fuselage had been strengthened. The aircraft was re-designated the D.III, but there was virtually no difference in performance between D.II and D.III. There were some minor external differences such as a deep chord on the engine cowling allowing extra cooling and an improved engine mounting. The additional weight caused the undercarriage to be strengthened, making the 'rakish look' disappear.

Fokker D.II, probably 528/16 of Jasta 16b which was interned in Switizerland

Fokker D.II Specifications	
Description:	Single-seat fighter/scout
Wing Span:	29ft. 8ins.
Wing Area:	194 sq. ft.
Length:	21ft.
Height:	8ft 4ins.
Weight Empty	844lbs
Weight Loaded:	1,267lbs
Engine:	One 100-hp Oberursel U.I, 9-cylinder, rotary
Maximum Speed:	93mph
Armament:	One fixed Spandau machine gun synchronised to fire through the propeller

Fokker D.III

The D.II was closely followed by the production model of the Fokker D.III at the end of August 1916. Almost immediately one of the aircraft was given to *Oberleutnant* Oswald Boelcke one of Germany's top aces. On the day after receiving the aircraft, September 2, 1916, Boelcke claimed his twentieth victim when he shot down a D.H2 flown by Captain R. Wilson. Encouraged by this Boelcke retained the

Fokker D.III. This appears to have been taken at the factory.

aircraft and during the next two weeks claimed five more victims.

In November 1916 in an effort to highlight any major, or indeed minor problems, a Fokker D.III, No. D.369/16, was tested to destruction. The results showed that the wing structure came up to the standard required, but the fuselage was 10 percent below the required strength. The rudders and elevators also failed to come up to the required standard and the control circuits displayed 23 percent more excessive friction than permitted, which in turn stretched the control cables too far. Modifications were made to the aircraft to bring it up to the required standard.

Between September 1916 and April 1917, 159 Fokker D.IIIs were delivered to the Army Flying Corps. Seven of those aircraft were operational on the Western Front by the end of September, a further thirty-four by January 1, but by the end of February only seven remained operational.

It is said that Ernst Udet, whilst flying the D.III, squeezed a dummy observer into the cockpit behind him, giving the impression that the tail was guarded by a rear gunner. The appearance of the D.III on the Front was short-lived as it was quickly realised that it was outclassed by the Albatros and the Halberstadt. Anthony Fokker was both furious and humiliated. He was convinced that his aircraft were far superior to the Albatros D.Is and D.IIs that dominated the fighter *Jastas*. He blamed Idflieg engineers for their undue criticism of his aircraft, the *Jasta* pilots at the Front for their inability to fly his aircraft to its full potential, in fact he blamed everyone except himself. He did not seem to realise that an operational aircraft was somewhat different to an ordinary aircraft. The stresses and strains put upon an operational aircraft during combat, set it aside from the normal model.

Although the Fokker D.III was easy to fly and very manoeuvrable, it was noticeably slower than the Nieuport and certainly no faster than the Sopwith 1 1/2 Strutter. This was not good enough for Boelcke so when the Albatros D.I appeared, a considerably better aircraft, Boelcke quickly switched allegiance. Without the support of Oswald Boelcke it was not long before the aircraft was withdrawn from frontline service. On Boelcke's recommendation, the Fokker D.III became a home-defence fighter and later was relegated to the flying schools. A total of 291 D.IIs and D.IIIs were built.

Fokker D.III Specifications	
Description:	Single-seat fighter/scout
Wing Span:	29ft. 8ins.
Length:	21ft.
Height:	7ft 5ins.
Weight Empty:	997lbs
Weight Loaded:	1,570lbs
Engine:	One 160-hp Oberursel U.III, 14-cylinder, rotary
Maximum Speed:	100mph
Armament:	Two fixed Spandau machine guns synchronised to fire through the propeller

Fokker D.IV

The Fokker D.IV also known as the Fokker M.20, was one of the aircraft said to have been designed by Anthony Fokker himself. Structural tests on the wings were carried out by German aeronautical engineers at Aldershof and serious weaknesses were found. The Idflieg insisted on improvements but again on further tests the structure of the wings became suspect. After a prolonged series of tests, it became apparent to Idflieg, that Fokker and his engineers relied heavily on guesswork when designing new aircraft and in reality the Fokker D.IV was no more than a reworked D.I. It had been modified to take the larger and heavier six-cylinder, in-line, water-cooled 160-hp Mercedes D.III engine and twin machine-guns together with their additional ammunition. However, Fokker had not taken into consideration the need to strengthen the structure of the fuselage and the wing spars.

Unhappy with the aircraft, engineers at Aldershof asked Fokker to attend further tests which infuriated him, angry at having his professional integrity questioned. To make matters worse, whilst there the wings collapsed when the sand loading reached 4.3 times the scheduled load - the permitted loading was five. Then a bolt that held the turnbuckle of a main bracing cable tore loose and upon closer examination, it was discovered that the turnbuckle did not even fit

The Fokker D.IV.

the cable. Fokker was humiliated, and after tests had revealed that the materials used should never have been used in any aircraft, let alone a military warplane, he received a severe reprimand for using inferior materials. Fokker returned to his factory fuming, convinced that it was not his fault but the fault of his engineers and designers.

Finally, with the modifications insisted on by Idflieg completed and the other minor problems ironed out, an initial order for twenty of the aircraft was placed, this was later increased to thirty.

The Fokker D.IV had some initial success but the aircraft was not liked by the front-line pilots and when a new engine became available, the 160-hp Mercedes D.IIIa, priority was given to have it installed in the Albatros and Pfalz fighters. To add insult to injury, Anthony Fokker was ordered to build 400 AEG C.IV two-seater aircraft under licence. Complaining that the complexity of the aircraft's design would prevent him making hardly any profit, Anthony Fokker was told to study the soundness of the aircraft's structural design and learn from it. During construction of the AEG C.IV, the whole Fokker factory was under the supervision of Dr Koner, an expert on materials and production control. One wonders if the reason for that was a deliberate move to enable the Idflieg to keep a watchful eye on Fokker.

Fokker D.IV Specifications	
Description:	Single-seat fighter/scout
Wing Span:	31ft. 10ins.
Length:	20ft. 8ins.
Height:	8ft 1ins.
Weight Empty:	1,340lbs
Weight Loaded:	1,850lbs
Engine:	One 160-hp Mercedes DIII, 6- cylinder, in-line, water-cooled
Maximum Speed:	100mph
Armament:	Two fixed Spandau machine guns synchronised to fire through the propeller

Fokker D.V

Just before his untimely death, designer Martin Kreutzer had been working on the replacement to the Fokker D.IV, the D.V. The final plans were finished by his successor Reinhold Platz and the D.V made its debut in September 1916. There were a number of differences, the 9-cylinder 100-hp Oberursel U.I engine was enclosed in a circular cowling, replacing the horseshoe shaped original cowling and had a large, blunt spinner fitted over the propeller's hub. The cowling was faired into the fabric covered, steel-tubed, box-girder fuselage, which narrowed down to a horizontal knife-edge to which the 'comma-shaped' tail was attached. The wings were slightly staggered and the upper wing, with a large angular centre-section cut out, was mounted close to the fuselage. This

Fokker D.V. 681/16

gave the pilot an excellent forward and upper view. The D.V was armed with a single fixed synchronised LMG 08 machine-gun mounted on top of the fuselage in front of the engine cowling. The ammunition box that fed the machine-gun was fitted inside the cockpit close to the pilot's knees, making the tight-fitting cockpit even more so.

A line-up of D.V's, probably at a Jastaschule

At the end of October 1916, Fokker sent the Fokker D.V, No. 2710/16, to Aldershof for tests, but like its predecessor, the Fokker D.IV, it failed. The wings collapsed when subjected to a load factor of 4.0 when the accepted tolerance was not less than 5.0. Fokker was distraught but, once again, he had only himself to blame. Prior to the aircraft being sent to Aldershof, Reinhold Platz had pleaded with Fokker to let him test the wing strength in their new experimental workshop. But typical of the arrogance of Fokker he refused, berating Platz for casting doubts on his engineering abilities.

Idflieg insisted that the wings were strengthened before being submitted for structural testing again. New strengthened wings with modified spars were quickly constructed and shipped to Aldershof for testing. The tests were satisfactory and the aircraft was accepted. Fokker conceded that the new experimental workshop at Schwerin greatly reduced the chances of rejection and would be used prior to all new aircraft be sent for testing.

Although the structural tests were deemed to be satisfactory, criticism was still levelled at the friction in the control circuits and the continuing problem of stretched control cables. What Anthony Fokker did not seem to realise, was that all his test flights were in short hops lasting no more than twenty minutes. Fighter pilots at the Front made, on an average, three to four flights per day all lasting more than one hour, and invariably their aircraft were being subjected to the strains of combat.

The Idflieg recommended the Fokker D.V for production, saying that it had all the hallmarks of a good fighter aircraft, indeed it was without doubt the best aircraft that Fokker had built to date. The German Navy became interested in the aircraft after hearing the reports and ordered a number of them. Inevitably they turned out to be unsatisfactory and, after a number of crashes, were scrapped. There wasn't a great welcome from the Army pilots who preferred the tried and tested Albatros D. III. It was however regarded as an excellent machine for training fighter pilots and as such were sent to training units. In one instance, just prior to receiving the first of the Fokker Dr.I Triplane, the *Richthofen Geschwader* took two of the D.Vs and made all the pilots fly the aircraft prior to flying the triplane. It was deemed that if they could fly the rotary powered Fokker D.V, they would have no problem flying the Dr.I Triplane.

The Army placed an order for twenty Fokker D.Vs, the first three being delivered in January 1917. By the end of the month the number had risen to thirty, twenty-five of which were operational. A total of 216 D.Vs were built, but very few ever saw service of the Western and Eastern Fronts.

At Fokker there seemed to be a dearth of ideas, so Reinhold Platz approached Anthony Fokker with a suggestion that he be allowed to design a new aircraft based on his own ideas. Anthony Fokker jumped at the suggestion and allowed Platz to select twenty of the best workers together with the best foreman and one draughtsman. With his team and fully equipped workshop, Platz set about building some experimental variants of the M.22 or Fokker D.V. The object was to take the best of all the variants and produce a top class aircraft. One of the first variants showed the diagonal member in the centre-section struts in the opposition direction to those of the D.V. Another model had more stringers fitted in the fuselage, had differently arranged bracing cables and had the front legs of its undercarriage faired.

A two-bay, long-span variant was built, and was known as the Fokker M.17z or streamlined Fokker D.II. It was in reality a D.V fuselage with a pair of warping wings from a D.II. It was powered by a nine-cylinder 110-hp Siemens-Sh. II bi-rotary engine. The cylinders of the engine only rotated at between 800 and 900 rpm, so required a larger diameter propeller, which in turn necessitated an extended undercarriage. There was also a need to alter the air intakes by cutting extra slots into the cowling. It was armed with twin fixed, forward-firing synchronised LMG.08/15 machine-guns. The aircraft was a pure experimental model and was never put into production.

Anthony Fokker himself was becoming more and more of an industrialist. He had purchased two piano factories in which Fokker aircraft components were made, the *Perzina Pianoforte Fabrik* and the *Pianoforte Fabrik Nuetzmann*. He had also acquired majority share holdings in the *Oberursel Motoren-Werke* and had become a director of the *Ungarische Allgemeine Maschinenfabrik AG* of Budapest. In addition he had become a naturalized German, although in his biography he claimed that he had been pressurized into becoming a German citizen and had also been threatened with military service. This is highly unlikely as the Germans most certainly did not want to upset a neutral Dutch government over a Dutchman whose only apparent interest in the German war effort was for how much money he could get out of it. However, there was a certain prestige for the Germans in having a rapidly-becoming-famous aircraft designer, choosing to give up his natural citizenship to become a German national.

Fokker D.V Specifications	
Description:	Single-seat fighter/scout
Wing Span:	28ft. 8ins.
Length:	19ft. 10ins.
Height:	7ft 6ins.
Weight Empty:	800lbs
Weight Loaded:	1,250lbs
Engine:	One 100-hp Oberursel UI, 9-cylinder, rotary
Maximum Speed:	106mph
Armament:	One fixed Spandau machine gun synchronised to fire through the propeller

Fokker Dr.I

In June 1917, with air superiority in the Flanders sector slipping rapidly from their grasp, the Imperial German Air Force put together four of their top *Jagdstaffeln*, Nos. 4, 6, 10 and 11. to form the first *Jagdgeschwader Nr. 1.* (Fighter Wing). Its commander was the legendary Manfred *Freiherr* von Richthofen - the Red Baron.

It was hoped that this crack fighter wing would be able to move rapidly between sectors and take on the Allied fighters, but it was obvious from the remarks made by the German pilots that they thought their aircraft inferior to those of the RFC (Royal Flying Corps). The German pilots were up against Sopwith Pups, Triplanes, Camels, S.E.5s, SPADs, Nieuports and Bristol Fighters. The Allied list of fighter aircraft was long, whilst the German pilots relied heavily on the Albatros as their front-line fighter.

Anthony Fokker had earlier visited von Richthofen whilst he was the commander of *Jasta* 11 and had seen the Sopwith Triplane in action against his own aircraft. Richthofen's technical officer, *Leutnant* Krefft, had pointed out

Manfred von Richthofen being strapped into his Fokker Dr.1 Triplane No.163/16 ready for a sortie.

the need for a similar aircraft and one that was needed quickly. Fokker and his designer Reinhold Platz set to work to develop a triplane that had the manoeuvrability and speed to out perform the best of the Allied fighters. Platz had never seen the Sopwith Triplane so the only description of what it looked like is what was given to him by Anthony Fokker. It is fair to say, therefore, that the resulting design for the Fokker Dr.1 was not unduly influenced by that of the

The V.3 the first prototype for the Fokker triplane. This prototype had no bracing struts on the wings and this caused extreme vibrations.

Sopwith Triplane. The result of the design was the Fokker V.3.

The capture of a Sopwith Triplane and the subsequent testing of it, convinced the Germans that a fighter based on a similar design would go a long way in regaining their air superiority.

Werner Voss, the leader of *Jasta* 10, regarded all British fighters superior to those of the German Air Force, a view supported by *Leutnant* Wilhelm Groos deputy leader of *Jasta* 11. The shooting down and wounding of Manfred von Richthofen on 6 July 1917, gave an unofficial endorsement to the need of a new fighter.

The three wings of the V.3 were staggered, as were the wings on the Sopwith

The Fokker V.4 incorporated wing struts to correct vibration.

Triplane, but it was the need for the pilot to get a good forward view that dictated the design. The development of the wings was the cause of some concern to Platz. The middle wing, which was situated in front of the cockpit, had two wing spars that were bridged top and bottom producing a box structure with four vertical webs and four narrow flanges. This unique arrangement did away with the need for internal drag bracing and allowed the wings to be simply covered with fabric.

After the first flight test, by Aldershof test pilots, Anthony Fokker insisted that balanced ailerons and elevators were fitted. A new, stronger middle wing with an increased span was also fitted. Then after a series of tests by test pilots in which they had subjected the Fokker V.3 to terminal nose dives, the wings were re-designed. The top and bottom wings were of a greater span than that of the middle wing, and bracing struts were added at the end of the wings to stop, or greatly reduce, any vibration. The incorporation of these features created the Fokker V.4.

The Fokker V.4 or Dr.1 as it became known, passed all its structural tests and on 26 August 1917, General Erich Ludendorf went to Aldershof to see the new fighter for himself. The aircraft was demonstrated by Anthony Fokker himself

Oberleutnant *Werner Voss taxiing out in his Fokker Dr.1 Triplane.*

and so impressed was Ludendorf that he ordered seventeen of the aircraft to be supplied as soon as possible.

Three days later the leader of *Jasta* 10, *Leutnant* Werner Voss made the first operational flight in the Dr.1, No. 103/17, and was delighted with the little fighter. The following day he had the opportunity to see how the aircraft responded under combat conditions, and is said to have shot down a SPAD, but there is no record of it. Between 30 August and 23 September 1917, Voss

Fokker Dr.1 Triplane of Jasta *10.*

accounted for 21 Allied aircraft, and was flying No. 103/17 when he met what he though was a lone S.E.5a. Diving into attack he suddenly realised that the S.E.5a was not alone and was himself attacked by four other S.E.5as. Among the Allied pilots was Captain James McCudden and 2/Lt Rhys David, both 'aces' and although Werner Voss fought with great tenacity and skill, he was eventually shot down.

Just after being released from hospital, Manfred von Richthofen flew the Fokker Dr.1, No. 102/17, for the first time. He had an instant rapport with the aircraft and on 1 September, just hours after having his first flight, he took to the air again and shot down an R.E.8 near Zonnebeke. The following day he requested that his entire *Jagdegeschwader* be re-equipped with the Fokker Dr.1 Triplane. Just two weeks later that same aircraft, 102/17, was destroyed when,

Rittmeister *Manfred von Richthofen with pilots of* Jagdstaffel 5. *Von Richthofen is seen talking to Joachim von Hippel* (nearest centre).

flown by *Oberleutnant* Kurt Wolff of *Jasta* 11, it was shot down after a battle with Sopwith Camels of No. 10 (N) Squadron.

In the middle of October 1917, six new Fokker Dr.1 Triplanes were delivered to Richthofen's *Geschwader*. There was one slight modification and that was the addition of wing-tip skids on the lower wings. Then certain problems started to manifest themselves. In the next batch of Fokker Dr.1 Triplanes was No. 115/17 which was delivered to *Jasta* 15 on 27 October 1917. The aircraft was placed in the experienced hands of *Leutnant* Heinrich Gontermann, holder of the *Orden Pour le Mérite*, when during a demonstration of aerobatics with the aircraft at a height of 1,500 ft., the top part of the wing started to break up and come away. The aircraft spun out of control killing Gontermann as it crashed into the ground. Two days later a similar incident involving a *Leutnant* Pastor happened, but this time it was witnessed by Manfred von Richthofen. Almost immediately

Fokker Dr.1 Triplane with 1914 crosses on the fuselage and tail.

von Richthofen ordered an enquiry and found that after the remains of both aircraft had been examined, bad workmanship was the main cause, aggravated by pressure to produce the aircraft at short notice.

The *ZAK Sturtz Kommission* which had been set up to examine all the facts, gave a warning to Fokker to improve his standard of workmanship immediately and furnished him with a list of modifications to be made to his Dr.1. This brought the entire Fokker factory to a standstill and the military authorities refused to accept any more aircraft from the company until the required modifications had been made to the wings and accepted by them.

A number of the modifications had already been made by Platz when he heard of the Kommission's findings, but some of the suggested modifications he thought were not necessary. It is interesting to note, that had the Kommission at the time spoken to Platz, they would have realised that Anthony Fokker was not the great designer of these aircraft as was thought, it was Reinhold Platz. This would have explained to them why, when asked a number of technical questions about the design of the Dr.1, Anthony Fokker stumbled about for answers.

The Fokker company was in trouble. They had an order for 320 of the triplanes, but had to use all existing profits to cover the cost of stripping down the wings and carrying out the required modifications. By the end of November

Hauptmann *Adolf Ritter von Tutschek, OC* Jagdgeschwader *2 preparing to take off from Foulis airfield.*

1917 the work had been completed and the results of the tests had come back from Aldershof. The final meeting, consisting of 27 senior officers and engineers, cleared the way for the Fokker Dr.1 Triplane production line to be re-started - the Fokker Dr.1 was back in full production.

Its appearance at the Front gave the German pilots a new impetus to take on the Allied fighters. They all took to the aircraft immediately, full of praise for its handling abilities and flying qualities. Even the history of wing failures didn't dampen their enthusiasm. But there were shortcomings. The Fokker Dr.1 was substantially better than the Sopwith Triplane which was coming to the end of

Fokker Dr.1 Triplane of Leutnant *Robert Tüxen of* Jasta 6.

its operational life, but compared to the D.H.4, D.H.9 and Bristol Fighters, it could not match any of them for speed and, in addition, the Allied aircraft could now fly and fight at higher altitudes than ever before. In short the Fokker Dr.1 Triplane was not the fighter aircraft that it was held up to be, and there were still the occasional incidents concerning the wing structure collapsing. A number of pilots were also expressing concern over the low powered 110-hp Le Rhône engine and moves were made to replace it with a more powerful model. But, before this could be implemented the aircraft was superseded and withdrawn before any further tests could be carried out.

On 12 December 1917, a Fokker Dr.1 Triplane, No.144/17 flown by *Leutnant* Stapenhorst of *Jasta* 11, came down in British held territory. The pilot had been wounded by anti-aircraft fire and brought the aircraft down to a near-perfect landing and, as the aircraft was undamaged, it was immediately spirited away for evaluation. The 'official' report stated that the design was one of the poorest of all German aircraft designs and had major structural weaknesses. Interestingly enough, after the war, a number of British and American pilots had the opportunity to fly the Fokker Dr.1 Triplane and were astonished at the control responses and agility of the aircraft. The official test reports have never been found, so one wonders whether or not it was a deliberate ploy by the Air

Fokker Dr.I

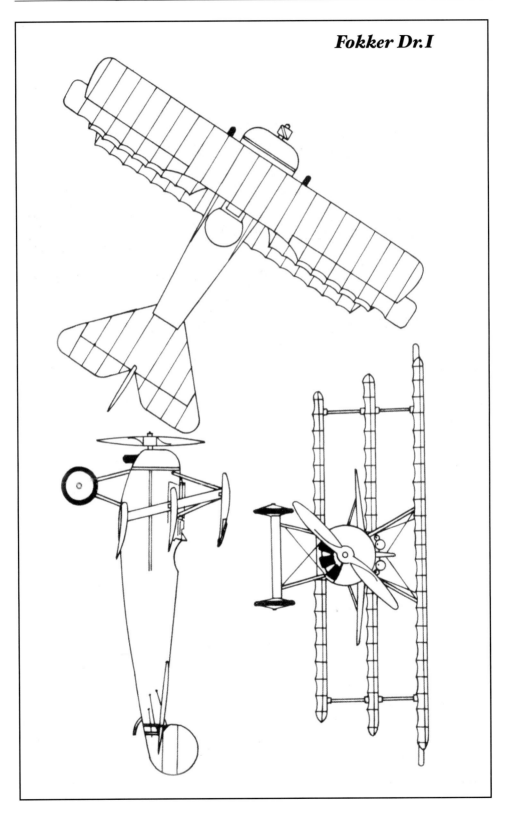

Fokker Triplane of Jasta 19 *being serviced. Note the reverse swastika on the fuselage which in this case was a squadron marking.*

Ministry to play down the aircraft's qualities.

During the aerial battle over Le Cateau, on 18 March 1918, over 60 German single-seater fighters took part, the vast majority of which were Fokker Dr.1 Triplanes. Among these pilots was Manfred von Richthofen, who, contrary to popular belief, flew an aircraft that was perfectly standard and had no additional machine-guns as was widely believed. He did however have the advantage of having at least two spare aircraft on standby in the event that his aircraft developed a problem - both painted red. He occasionally attached leader's streamers to his wing spars after, it is said, a British pilot, who had been shot down by Richthofen, had looked in vain for the legendary 'Red Baron' as a most desirable target, but couldn't find him. Richthofen felt that Prussian pride would be offended if he didn't rise to the challenge and fitted the streamers.

The search for a new engine for the Fokker Dr.1 continued, and towards the end of 1917 the Fokker sponsored Oberursel UR.II engine was accepted by the German military. At the same time the new 160-hp eleven-cylinder counter-rotating Sh.3 engine built by Siemens and Halske had just been completed. A much more powerful engine than the Le Rhône, the Sh.3 was still in the experimental stage but already the military were showing interest. Fokker, desperate that the Sh.3 did not take the place of the Oberursel UR.II, did everything he could to block trials of the engine in his aircraft. In the end the military decided to step in and took control of all the trials, but before any new engine could be fitted into the triplane it had been superseded by the Fokker D.VII biplane.

Fokker Dr.I Triplane Specifications	
Description:	Single-seat fighter/scout
Wing Span:	23ft. 7ins.
Length:	18ft. 11ins.
Height:	9ft 8ins.
Weight Empty:	895lbs
Weight Loaded:	1,290lbs
Engine:	110-hp Oberursel URII or a Thulin built Le Rhône, 9-cylinder, rotary
Maximum Speed:	103mph
Armament:	Twin fixed Spandau machine guns synchronised to fire through the propeller. They could also be fired independantly

Fokker D.VI.

Fokker D.VI

Fokker continued with the D series with the development of the D.VI. The first experimental type, the V.13, was fitted with the 110-hp Oberursel UR.II rotary engine, but it was soon realised that it had insufficient power. It had a climb rate of 550 feet per minute and an operating ceiling of 18,500 feet, which for combat purposes was not good enough. In May 1918, a 145-hp Oberursel UR.III was fitted into the D.VI and although there was some improvement it still never quite measured up. Nevertheless, by July 1918, twenty-one of the aircraft were in operational use, followed two months later by a further six.

The Austrian Army bought seven D.VIs without any acceptance flights. The fact that the aircraft was already in operational use was probably good enough for them, although there were two modification made. Their aircraft differed from the German model inasmuch as they had a fixed synchronised Schwarzlose machine-gun mounted on the fuselage in front of the engine cowling and a manually operated Mannlicher machine gun mounted on the upper wing.

In total sixty Fokker D.VIs were supplied to the German Army before being superseded by the D.VII.

Fokker D.VII

Whilst the production lines for the D.VI were turning over, the prototype D.VII, in the shape of the V.11, was being evaluated. In March 1918, the aircraft passed the structural tests comfortably, Anthony Fokker had learnt from previous experience the need for patience and care. During upper wing tests at

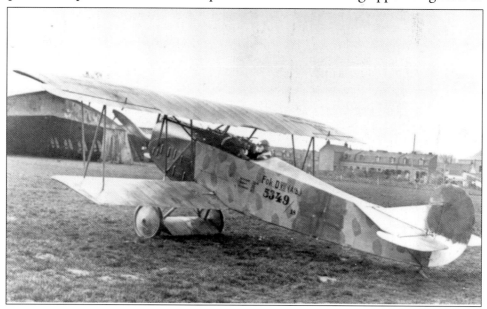

An Albatros built Fokker D.VII.

Aldershof the wing loading reached 10.52 (the required load factor being 5.0) before a joint on the interplane strut failed. This made the Fokker D.VII the strongest German operational aircraft built during the First World War and not one structural failure in the air was recorded on the D.VII. Dive tests were carried out and again the D.VII showed no signs of weakness. But there was a problem and it was discovered quite by accident. When moist sand had been used the leading edges of the wings deformed. This led to wrapping the plywood ribs in wet cloths for twenty-four hours, after which it was found when a load factor was applied, they collapsed. Further experiments on the plywood discovered that the wood being used was substantially inferior to that be used by other aircraft manufacturers.

Anthony Fokker was once again brought up before the Idflieg and once again he was warned about the use of inferior materials. A more detailed examination of the aircraft took place. It was found that the control column was not strong enough, the rudder bar was unable to withstand the prescribed load factor, the anchoring of the fuel tank became suspect as did the undercarriage. The control cables once again came under scrutiny and it was suspected that they were not being pre-stretched. Modifications were insisted upon and after all had been done the aircraft was deemed to be ready for operational use.

A number of engines were tried in the D.VII, but the two that were chosen were the 185-hp BMW (*Bavarian Motor Werke*) IIIa and the six-cylinder, in-line 160-hp Mercedes. The pilots were delighted with the new aircraft and its engine and initially ninety-two of the D.VIIs with the BMW engine were supplied to

Fokker D.VIIs of JG3 at Nivelles

All-white Fokker D.VII belonging to Oberleutnant *Hermann Göring when he was* Jasta Führer *of* Jagdgeschwader *1. Hermann Göring is sitting in the cockpit.*

the Army. So popular was the aircraft, that the *Albatros Werke* at Schneidemühl started to build the aircraft under licence. The unit to receive the first Fokker D.VIIs was *Jagdgeschwader* I commanded by the legendary Manfred von Richthofen. Within two months *Jagdstaffeln* 26, 27, 2, 36 and 3 were supplied with the aircraft an, by the end of November 1918, the home defence units, a total of forty-seven *Jagdstaffeln*, had been equipped with 775 Fokker D.VIIs.

The Fokker D.VIIs arrival on the Western Front was greeted by the Allies with some scepticism, its lack of graceful lines gave the impression of a lumbering lump of metal and wood. Then the Allied pilots discovered that this lumbering aircraft was not what it seemed. Those who encountered the aircraft in combat soon found out that it had a surprising turn of speed and could outclimb most of the other types of fighter. It also had the ability to attack two-seaters from below and pour a stream of bullets into the underside of its adversary.

There was one area that was the cause of some concern and that was the overheating of the aluminium ammunition boxes. Several incidents were reported, one on 15 July 1918, caused the death of its pilot *Leutnant* Friedrich. The aircraft was on patrol when the whitish smoke of burning phosphorus was seen to billow from the cockpit. *Leutnant* Friedrich jumped from his now burning aircraft, but his parachute failed to open and he was killed. The following day there was a similar incident, only this time the pilot's parachute opened. There were a number of similar incidents that resulted in the banning of the use of incendiary ammunition in the Fokker D.VII until a solution was found.

One of the variants of the Fokker D.VII, was that of a two-seater. By removing

Pilots of Jasta *10*, Jagdgeschwader *1. L-R:*Uffz. *Hennig;* Ltn. *Schibilsky;* Ltn. *Grassman;* Ltn.
Heldman: Offstvtr *Aue;* Ltn. *Kohlbach;* Uffz. *Klamt;* Ltn. *Bähren. All the pilots are wearing
Heinecke parachute harness. In the background can be seen some of the Fokker D.VII aircraft.*

the guns and ammunition boxes and fitting the undercarriage fuel tank of the
V-36, an extra seat could be installed. An additional fuel tank was installed
between the two cockpits. There were only two models constructed and after
extensive evaluation tests, it was decided that the observers cockpit was too
cramped for observation and infantry liaison duties.

When one of the Fokker D.VIIs fell into the hands of the Allies, they carried

Line-up of Jagdstaffel *26 Fokker Dr.1 Triplanes. The pilot in the foreground is* Leutnant
Otto Esswein.

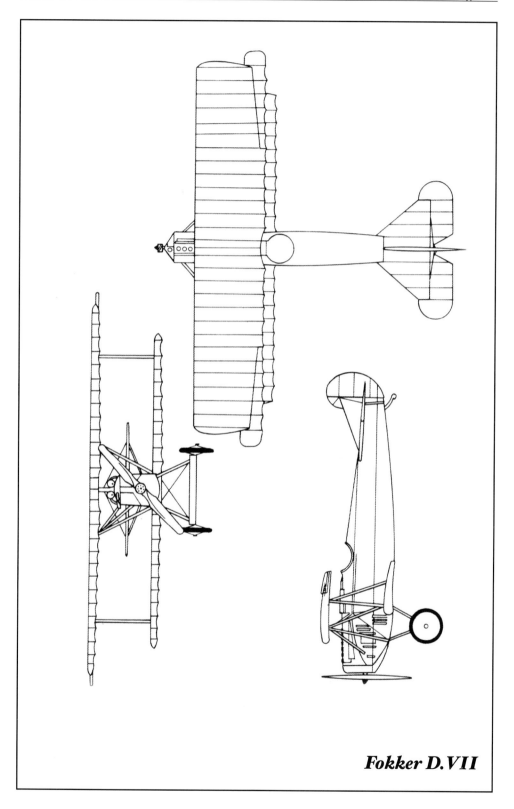

Fokker D.VII

out an in-depth examination of the engine and the aircraft. Their report showed a high regard for the aircraft, which was endorsed by a paragraph in the Armistice conditions that demanded the immediate surrender of all the Fokker D.VII types.

Fokker E.V - D.VIII

The last of the Fokker D series was the Fokker D.VIII, based on the V.26 design. Initially the aircraft had been designated the Fokker E.V as single-wing aircraft had always carried the 'E' prefix. Idflieg, however, had recently issued an order that all single-seater fighter aircraft should now be placed in the D series category.

The Fokker E.V (D.VIII) as supplied to Jasta 6.

There had been problems earlier with the wing loading on the Fokker E.V but this was said to have been resolved and the Fokker D.VIII, as it was now called, made its first appearance with *Jasta 6* of *Jagdgeschwader I* and some weeks later with *Jasta 19* of *Jagdgeschwader II*. Initially the pilots were extremely enthusiastic about the little single-seater fighter, but then one of the old major problems that had dogged Fokker in the past raised its head again - the suspect wing. During a familiarization flight on 16 August 1918, *Leutnant* Ernst Riedel's V.III of *Jasta 19*, lost part of its starboard wing and the pilot was killed. Three days later another of the aircraft flown by *Leutnant* Emil Rolff of *Jasta 6*, was killed when his wing broke up just after take-off. The wreckage of both aircraft were subjected to detail examination at Aldershof by Idflieg engineers who, came to the conclusion that Anthony Fokker had lapsed back into his old ways and was using inferior materials. Fokker was summoned to Aldershof and told

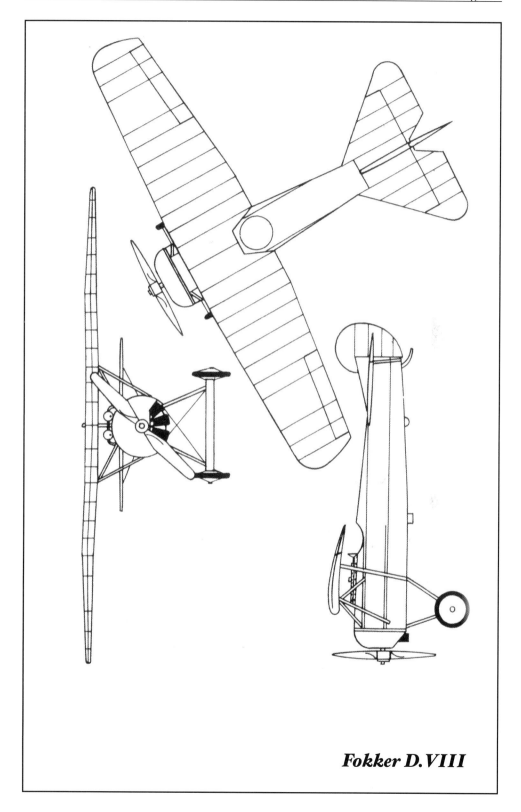

Fokker D.VIII

that all D.VIII aircraft were to be grounded and their wings returned to Fokker to be replaced with new wings using the standards set by Idflieg.

Fokker, in his usual arrogant manner, tried to lay the blame squarely at the feet of Idflieg's engineers, saying that they had got the requirements all wrong and he had just followed them. But when he discovered that Idflieg had been considering preparing criminal charges against him for fraudulent transactions against the German government, and in doing so had placed the lives of German pilots at risk, he quickly conceded to their demands. Within two months new wings were on their way back to the various *Jastas*, all constructed to the exact requirements of Idflieg.

A number of the new aircraft were assigned to *Jagdstaffel* 11 commanded by *Oberleutnant* Ernst Udet, on 24 October 1918. Three other units were also equipped at the same time, *Jagdstaffeln* 1 and 23, and also the German Navy's *Marine Land-Jagdgruppe Sachsenberg* of which *Oberleutnant zur See* Theodor Osterkamp commanded *Jagdgeschwader* 51.

The Fokker D.VIII, a cantilever designed parasol monoplane, was powered by a nine-cylinder 110-hp Oberursel U II rotary engine which gave it a top speed of 127mph. A total of 381 Fokker D.VIIIs had been delivered to the Army and Navy by the time of the Armistice, yet in this relatively short time, the D.VIII had gained a reputation and had shown itself to have been an aircraft that was technically well advanced. Yet, surprisingly enough, only two recorded victories are said to have been achieved by the aircraft. The first by *Leutnant* Emil Rolff on 16 August 1918 (only three days before he was to die due to wing failure), when he shot down a Sopwith Camel D9595 of 203 Squadron, RAF flown by Sergeant P.M.Fletcher. The other was after the war on 29 April 1919, when Lieutenant Stefan Stec of No.7 Squadron, Polish Air Force, shot down a Ukrainian Nieuport.

Fokker D.VIII Specifications	
Description:	Single-seat fighter/scout
Wing Span:	27ft. 4ins.
Length:	19ft. 3ins.
Height:	9ft 3ins.
Weight Empty:	890lbs
Weight Loaded:	1,330lbs
Engine:	One 110-hp Oberursel UII
	9-cylinder rotary
Maximum Speed:	127mph
Armament:	Twin Spandau synchronised to
	fire through the propeller.

Eighty-five Fokker D.VIII were operational on the Western Front and twenty more with the Naval coast-defence units by the end of the war. Not one fell into the hands of the Allies during this period, but at the end of the war a large number were flown over the border into Holland. The Dutch Army installed the nine-cylinder 145-hp Oberursel UR.III engine into the aircraft and used them for a number of years.

CHAPTER TWO

S.E.5 and 5a

In 1915 a new French aero-engine appeared, it was designed by Marc Birkigt and made by the Hispano-Suiza company. The design incorporated an eight-cylinder water-cooled 'vee' unit with each bank of cylinders cast in aluminium as a one-piece block. It delivered 150-h.p. for a weight of only 445-h.p.

One of these engines was inspected in Paris, during the Summer of 1915, by Lieutenant-Colonel H.R.M. Brooke-Popham. On his recommendation a British order for fifty engines was placed in August 1915 and negotiations were begun for the manufacture of the engine in Britain. These negotiations involved the parent Hispano-Suiza company in Barcelona as well as the French firms who were manufacturing the engine under contract and cost a great deal of time. British production of the Hispano-Suiza did not begin until the spring of 1916.

With the promise of this compact and workmanlike engine being available the design staff at Farnborough began work on the design of a new single seat fighter which was given the designation of S.E.5. Their aim was to produce an aeroplane which could be flown with reasonable safety by pilots who had only sketchy flying training of the period. This presupposed a certain degree of inherent stability and the design was revised after early wind tunnel tests had shown that the original concept would not have been sufficiently stable.

The design work was largely done by H.P.Folland assisted by J.Kenworthy and Major Frank W.Goodden. Much of the later success of the S.E.5 is attributable to careful designing, particularly in the matter of detail design at which Folland excelled.

The machine's basic structure was typical of the war period. The fuselage was a wire braced box girder composed of wooden longerons and spacers. Plywood was applied to the fuselage sides below the engine bearers and extended as far aft as the front spar of the lower mainplanes. A flat car type radiator was mounted at the nose and the short exhaust manifolds had a single central outlet. The main fuel tank was mounted on top of the upper longerons behind the engine. The tank was shaped to the contour of the fuselage top decking. On the prototype S.E.5 the tank was covered by an extended engine cowling but it was left uncowled in production machines. There was gravity tank mounted externally above the centre section well out to port. The undercarriage was a simple structure consisting of two steel tube eves.

S.E.5a, D6940 'Parish of Inch No.2' of No.29 Squadron. Pilot Lt C M Wilson.

The wings had spruce spars and were braced internally by wire. There was no conventional compression struts and in their place were certain ribs which were made solid. The single bay interplane bracing was supplemented by two auxiliary mid-bay flying wires on each side. The incidence of the tailplane could be varied in flight and a rather unusual feature was the location of the elevator cable runs within the fuselage and tailplane. The vertical tail assembly was a characteristic structure of the highly practical design.

The fifty Hispano-Suiza engines which had been ordered in 1915 were delivered between August and December 1916. One of the first was installed in the prototype S.E.5, A.4561, which flew in December 1916. This machine was

S.E.5a, serial B603. Note extended exhaust pipe

S.E.5, serial A4561, first prototype following modifications.

later flown with modified exhausts and side extensions of the windscreen. In its first flights the S.E.5 gave every indication of being a satisfactory aircraft, but structural failure of the wings brought about the destruction of the prototype at the end of January 1917. In the crash Frank Goodden lost his life, a life which could be ill spared from Britain's aeronautical effort of the time.

Production had already been initiated but was suspended while the crash was investigated. The shape of the wing tip was redesigned to be much less sharply raked. Also a modified strut to the spar joints was fitted and stronger lift bracing introduced. Construction of the first production batch of S.E.5s was too far advanced for the new wing tip shape to be used but the spars were

S.E.5 with the Hispano-Suiza engine, circa 1917

reinforced and the other modifications incorporated. The machines of the second batch of S.E.5s had the modified wings of reduced span which became standard on all subsequent S.E.5s. Some machines were fitted with an improved gravity tank which was mounted within the leading edge of the upper centre section. This arrangement also became standard.

The modifications proved to be entirely satisfactory and in service the S.E.5 airframe gained a reputation for great structural strength which inspired confidence in combat.

Armament fitted to production machines consisted of two machine guns. A Vickers gun was mounted in front of the cockpit on the port side and with its breech mechanism enclosed within the top decking. A Lewis gun was carried above the centre section on a Foster mounting. The latter weapon could slide back and along a curved rail until it was nearly vertical and in this position it could be reloaded and fired upwards. It has been said that the Lewis gun was fitted to the S.E.5 in this way because Captain Albert Ball, V.C. exploited its

S.E.5 as of No.29 Squadron, Oudezeele, August 1918.

ability to fire upwards.

The Vickers gun on the S.E.5 was synchronised to fire through the revolving airscrew by means of the Constantinesco hydraulic synchronising gear. This gear gave a good deal of trouble before it became understood. Frequently the Vickers would not fire or, if it did, an S.E. pilot might find that he had shot his own airscrew off. Major J.T.B.McCudden experienced these troubles despite meticulous personal attention to his guns. Describing his combat experiences at a time as late as September 1917 he wrote, "My word. You cannot realise what it is to get on the Hun's tail time after time and then have your guns let you down".

The first production S.E.5s were completed in March 1917 and delivered to

No.56 Squadron. That unit had been formed at Gosport in June 1916 from a nucleus provided by No.28 Squadron, and moved to London Colney during the following month. Major R.G.Blomfield assumed command early in February 1917 and on the 26th Captain Albert Ball was posted to the squadron as a Flight Commander. No.56 Squadron received its first S.E.5 on March 13th 1917 and by April 5th its establishment of new machines was complete. On that date an advanced party went to France and two days later the complete squadron arrived at Vert Galand aerodrome.

In one or two features the S.E.5 was not satisfactory for operational use, and Major Blomfield kept his squadron grounded for two weeks to allow some essential modifications to be made. The machines delivered to No.56 Squadron had a cumbersome transparent windshield which extended forward over the

Legend on fuselage states- 'Huns 29 in 14 days'. No.85 Squadron, St Omer, June 1918. Note ladies garter around flying helmet.

breech of the Vickers gun. It may have been hope that this 'greenhouse', as it was called by the pilots, would facilitate clearing of gun stoppages, but all it did was to interfere seriously with the pilot's forward view and it could have been a danger in a crash. Major Blomfield had the greenhouses replaced by a small flat Triplex windscreen which was adopted as a standard fitting on all S.E.5s.

Experience showed that it was better to have the fire of the Lewis gun converging with that of the Vickers at about 50 yards range instead of being parallel to it. The Foster mounting was therefore raised slightly at the rear end.

The S.E.5s of No.56 Squadron made their first patrol on April 22nd 1917 when five machines led by Ball patrolled between Lieven and Croisilles. An Albatros two seater which they pursued escaped destruction only because strict orders had been issued that no S.E.5 was to cross the lines in any circumstances.

Captain Ball scored his first victory on a S.E.5 on April 23rd when he shot down an Albatros scout in flames from 13,000 feet over Cambrai. Ball did not at first like the S.E.5 for it was less responsive than the sensitive Nieuport Scout which he had been flying. His dislike of the S.E was so great that he asked for, and obtained, a Nieuport for his personal use if No.56 Squadron. However, after being saved from death on April 26th 1917 by the speed and double fire power of the S.E.5 he realised its true worth and used his Nieuport only once more

S.E.5a F927 'A' of No.29 Squadron, Nickendorf.

over the lines.

Convincing proof of the S.E.5's great structural strength was provided on April 28th 1917. Lieutenant G.C.Maxwell had engaged a group of Albatros scouts over Fontaine when his machine was struck by anti-aircraft fire. His engine was damaged and elevator controls rendered almost totally ineffective. With little control over his fighter Maxwell glided down and hit the ground near Combles at about 140m.p.h. The engine and its bearers broke off but the remainder of the aircraft bounced on for nearly a hundred yards and was completely wrecked. Maxwell was uninjured.

Various experimental versions of the Hispano-Suiza engines were flown in S.E.5 airframes. In September 1917 engines with compression ratios increased to 5.3 to 1 and 5.6 to 1 were fitted. The latter engine developed 192-h.p. Finally in

S.E.5a, D6950.

December 1917 a Wolseley Viper engine was tested in an S.E.5. According to the official records of the performance all these installations were made in S.E.5s with long span wings.

The Hispano-Suiza engine underwent development during 1916 and a geared version was produced which developed 200h.p. The second S.E.5 prototype was fitted with one of these engines. This first installation was very similar to that of the 150-h.p. Hispano-Suiza and could be distinguished only by its higher thrust line and left hand airscrew. The aeroplane had the marginal form of S.E.5 wings with reinforced rear spars. The third prototype A.4563 was also fitted with the 200h.p. Hispano-Suiza but the radiator was provided with shutters and a four bladed airscrew. The shorter span wings were fitted and the exhausts were the L-

Production line of S.E.5as at the Wolesley factory. Viper engines.

Major A D Carter at Upper Heyford in his S.E.5a.

shaped manifolds which had been used on most of the first production S.E.5s This aircraft was used operationally in France by Squadrons No.56 and 84.

This modified version was designated S.E.5a and all subsequent machines were of this type. The first production S.E.5a was delivered to No.56 Squadron in June 1917 and thereafter the type gradually replaced the S.E.5. No.56 Squadron was re-equipped with the new type by August 1917. The S.E.5a fuselage forward of the cockpit was a little deeper than that of the S.E.5 and

S.E.5a, B83, built by the Air Navigation Co.

long horizontal exhaust pipes were standard fittings. In No.56 Squadron these long pipes were not liked at first and were cut off just behind the rear exhaust stub and replaced by short pipes welded on at an outwards angle. Later, however, the long pipes were used again.

Unfortunately the 200h.p. Hispano-Suiza engine was dogged by ill luck and consequently the S.E.5a was not so immediately effective as it might have been. Really large scale production was still some way off owing to the difficulty in obtaining engines. At the insistence of the Admiralty, the Air Board had ordered 8,000 Hispano-Suiza engines in November 1916, principally from the Mayen concern in France. This firm built a large factory for the purpose using some £2 million advanced by the British Government, but the first engines did not come off the lines until late 1917.

Meanwhile production of the 200h.p., engine was undertaken in England by the Wolseley company and other H-S engines made in France were fitted to S.E.5as.

The Wolseley built engines were not at first successful. On May 7th 1917 Sir William Weir, Controller of Aeronautical Supplies, had to report that a 200h.p. Hispano Suiza engine made by Wolseley had broken four successive crankshafts after an average run of only four hours. Trials of this engine continued and production went ahead after eleven modifications had been introduced but the delay led to a reduction in output. As a stop gap the Wolseley concern was asked to make 400 Hispano-Suiza engines of the original direct drive version, an order that was later increased to 1,100. However, it was apparently not been made clear to the contractors that they were required to produce the existing type for they set about developing from the 150-h.p. Hispano-Suiza a high compression engine of the same nominal power. This engine became known as

Rare two seat conversion. Serial D3554, CFS Upavon, 1918.

the Wolseley Viper, but the time spent on its design seriously retarded production by the company and did nothing to alleviate the immediate shortage of Hispano-Suiza engines, whereas it had been expected that 140 would have been delivered by the end of August 1917. Only ten had been completed.

This serious situation was further aggravated by the unreliability of the first 200h.p. Hispano-Suiza engines delivered from the French firm of Brasier. Failures were frequent and engines had to be sent to the Clement Talbot works for overhaul. One of the most serious defects lay in the faulty hardening of the gear wheels and airscrew shaft and they had to be replaced by British made spares. By October 1917, however, the shortage of engines had become so acute that some of the French Hispanos were passed into service with the original unevenly hardened gears. The engines were accepted by the Aeronautical Inspection Directorate only on direct written instructions, and cautionary entries in the engine log books should be carefully watched. In extenuation of this indefensible action it was pleased that defective engines were better than none at all.

These failures hit the S.E.5a particularly hard and by January 1918 no fewer

First, and only, Oxford-v- Cambridge air race held at Hendon, July 1921.

than 400 new S.Es were held up in stores because no engines were available for them. The set back could hardly have occurred at a more unfortunate time as airframe production had expanded greatly during the last quarter of 1917. During this period 604 S.E.s were produced whereas only 157 had been built during the preceding three months.

When in service the machines with the defective engines were bad for morale. No pilot could be reasonably expected to have confidence in a machine of known unreliability.

S.E.5a. Note machine gun on upper wing surface.

Fortunately the Admiralty's foresight in 1916 saved the situation which had become ugly indeed. In the early months of 1918 the first deliveries of Mayen-built Hispano-Suizas were made against the order for 8,000 engines.

In action the S.E.5a was an excellent fighting aircraft and its first testimonial lies in the fact that it was the mount of the leading British fighter pilots of the war. Major Edward (Mick) Mannock, V.C., D.S.O, M.C scored more than 50 of his 73 confirmed victories while flying an S.E.5a, and the type was also flown with signal success by such pilots as Bishop, McCudden, Beauchamp-Proctor, McElroy and Rhys-Davids. The S.E. though it had none of the hair trigger sensitivity of its great contemporary, the Sopwith Camel, was usefully

S.E.5a, F9029 built by Vickers.

manoeuvrable and yet stable enough to facilitate accurate shooting. Its reputation for strength was an enormous asset in combat for if it lacked anything in manoeuvrability that small deficiency was more than outweighed by the liberties which could be taken without fear of structural failure.

S.E.5as became available in increasing numbers throughout the summer of 1917 and were issued to several squadrons. Despite trouble with the engines and the Constantinesco gun gear the aircraft gave a good account of itself. On September 28, 1917 Captain J.T.R.McCudden of No.56 Squadron led is patrol of S.E.5as at attack a group of Albatros scouts over Boesinghe and destroyed five of the enemy without loss to the British machines.

McCudden had several S.E.5as while he was with No.56 Squadron. The first was B.519 and was followed by A.4863 which gave him a great deal of trouble, particularly with its Constantinesco gear. In October 1917 he took over the Martinsyde built S.E.5a B.35 after another pilot had discovered the strength of the S.E's construction by flying McCudden's previous machine through the side of a housed. The pilot concerned was unhurt. On December 3rd McCudden received B.4891, an S.E.5a built by the Royal Aircraft Factory.

The machine had a smaller fin than was standard and narrow-chord elevators

S.E.5a, C8904, aircraft 'H', No.29 Squadron, Bickendorf.

were fitted. It was one of the first S.E.5as to have the improved undercarriage with the strengthened forward leg in each vee. For a time B.4891 wore the spinner on an L.V.G. C.V that McCudden had shot down on November 30th 1917. It was painted Red and added 3m.p.h to the speed of the S.E.5a.

McCudden took the keenest interest in his S.E. and it was largely due to careful tuning that he was able to reach 20,000 feet in it, whereas the average Service S.E. could seldom exceed 17,000 feet. In January 1918 he had a specially modified Hispano-Suiza engine installed. It had a special high compression pistons and greatly improved the S.E.'s rate of climb.

S.E.5a in U.S national markings.

In squadron service the S.E.5a underwent various detail modifications to meet the personal requirements of pilots. Some machine were given extra bracing wires to the fin of mainplanes. Some S.E.5as of No. 24 Squadron were rigged with reduced dihedral in order to increase manoeuvrability and, most commonly, many aircraft had the streamlined headrest removed by pilots who wanted the best possible rearwards view.

The strengthened undercarriage mentioned above was introduced late in 1917. The forward leg of each 'vee', which on earlier S.Es had been a single steel tube of streamline section, was a built-up component consisting of two steel tubes in the form of a long slender inverted 'V'. The axle lay at the open end of this leg between the two steel tubes. The double leg was faired over with plywood or sheet metal.

As more powerful Hispano-Suiza engines became available they were installed in S.E.5as. The 220-h.p. and 240-h.p. geared H-S were fitted to some machines, and finally the Wolseley W.4a Viper was standardised for the type. The Viper was a high compression development of the Hispano-Suiza engine which was a direct drive engine and had a right hand airscrew. As has already stated the Viper was fitted to an S.E.5 airframe in December 1917.

The Viper installation in the S.E.5a was of distinctive appearance for the nose of the aircraft looked bulkier than with the Hispano-Suiza and was generally less streamlined. The sides of the radiator housing was quite flat, and short horizontal shutters were fitted to the radiator. Most Viper S.Es dispensed with fairings at the ends of the valve rocker housings of the engines.

A few S.E.5as were fitted with the Wolseley W.4B, an engine with the same nominal power as the Viper but with reduction gearing to the airscrew shaft.

During the German offensive of March 1918 much ground attack work was performed by the scout squadrons of the R.A.F. The S.E.5as of Nos. 24 and 84

Line-up of No.85 Squadron's S.E.5as, St Omer, 21 June 1918. The same fuselage emblem was used by the squadron in W.W.2 on its Hurricanes.

Squadrons did a considerable amount if this hazardous low flying duty and added low level bombing to their repertoire. Each S.E. carried four 25 lb Cooper bombs in racks under the fuselage. In the afternoon of March 22nd 1918 twelve S.E.5as of No. 84 Squadron dropped forty-five bombs on enemy troops and

S.E.5as of No.111 Squadron, Palestine, 1918. Cooper bomber under fuselage of nearest aircraft.

transport near to Holnon and scored many direct hits. The work of No. 24 Squadron between February and November 1918 can be assessed from the facts that their S.E.5as dropped 2,229 bombs and fired 95,522 rounds at ground targets. And so the S.E.5a flew and fought on until victory came in November. Several of the best German fighting pilots fell in combat with the S.Es among them Werner Voss, Kurt Wusthoff and Eric Loewenhardt. It was an aeroplane whose fighting qualities were recognised and respected by the enemy.

The S.E.5 had an early introduction to Home Defence duties. On June 13th the first enemy daylight attack on London was made with heavy loss of life. So great was public indignation over this attack that the Government instructed Sir Douglas Haig to send on fighting squadron home from France and one to Calais. No. 56 Squadron flew its S.E.5as to Bekesbourne on June 21st and remained there until July 5th having seen no enemy aircraft at all.

S.E.5a, D3540 'K' of No.40 Squadron. Pilot Capt. G.H. Lewis. Aircraft called 'The Artful Dodger'.

S.E.5as were issued to Home Defence squadrons but were not regarded as completely suitable for this class of work. They were satisfactory once they were in the air but the water cooled engine took much longer to warm up than did contemporary rotary engines, and quick take offs were not possible. The S.E.5a was also said to be difficult to land on small aerodromes at night. The four Home Defence Squadrons which had the type had all been re-equipped with Sopwith Camels by the time of the Armistice.

The S.E.5s served on other fronts in small numbers for it was with reluctance that the War Office permitted the dispatch of up to date aircraft to the less spectacular theatres of war. The Germans did not make the same mistake.

In September 1917 Lieutenant-General G.F.Milne, then in command of the British forces in Macedonia, wrote to the War Office and pressed for more aircraft to be placed at his disposal. On October 12th the War Office sanctioned an increase in the establishment of Squadrons Nos. 17 and 47 and stated that nine S.E.5as had been allocated. The first S.E. arrived early in November 1917 and by the following February each squadron had four. These machines had an immediate beneficial effect, and Captain F.G. Saunders and Lieutenant G.E.Gibbs of No. 17 Squadron made excellent use of their new mounts. On April 26th, 1918, the S.E.5as of Squadrons Nos. 17 ands 47 were handed over to No. 150 Squadron, a new fighting squadron which had been formed on April 1st.

A few S.E.5as were used in Mesopotamia by 'A' Flight of No. 72 Squadron, which had arrived at Basra on March 2nd, 1918.

For training purposes some S.E.5as were converted into two-seaters. A second cockpit was cut out in front of the normal one. It has been said, however, that the flying characteristics were badly impaired and that the two seat S.E.5a would spin at the slightest provocation.

Some S.E.5as were used for experimental purposes both during and after the war. At least one aircraft was fitted with an under-slung radiator in place of the

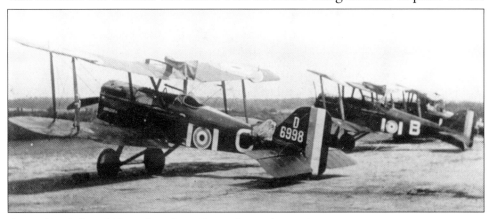

S.E.5a 'A' Flight6 of No.24 Squadron, Cappy, September 1918.

normally frontal surface, and the nose was covered in by a blunt fairing. The engine appeared to be a Wolseley Viper and the radiator apparently consisted of two Viper type radiator blocks laid on their sides and mounted, one above the other, to form a single radiator.

At Martlesham Heath the Viper powered S.E.5a, E.5923, was fitted with an experimental tail unit. The fin and rudder were elliptical and somewhat similar to the vertical tail assembly of the German D.F.W. C.V, while the tailplane was

S.E.5a of No.111 Squadron, Palestine.

tapered and sharply swept back. The tailplane was in two parts with the forward portion fixed, but the rear portion could be adjusted from the cockpit to provide longitudinal trimming. For spinning experiments another S.E.5a was fitted with a balanced rudder generally similar to that of the Avro 504. It was also fitted with two small fins on the tailplane.

R.600 was rigged with no dihedral for experimental manoeuvrability conducted at the R.A.E just after the war. C.1091 was fitted with the Royal Aircraft Factory variable pitch airscrew. Other experiments were conducted to investigate exhaust manifold temperatures and one S.E.5a was fitted with large finned pipes of cast aluminium for this purpose.

In the field of flight safety the S.E.5a was used to test automatic landing apparatus and fire extinguishing equipment. In 1919 one was fitted with a Palethorpe Skid, and in the following year a different type of ground proximity equipment was tested. Major G.H.Norman was responsible for the installation of a French fire prevention apparatus in an S.E.5a in 1921. This was almost certainly E.5927. To put this new equipment to the fullest test Norman set fire to his machine in the air. The extinguisher put the fire out. but smoke blinded Norman on the approach and he crashed. His injuries later proved to be fatal.

S.E.5as of No.40 Squadron, 1918.

Some S.E.5as remained in service after the war but it was soon withdrawn. Australia and Canada used the type and one Viper engined S.E.5a was taken to Japan in 1921 by the British Aviation Mission to the Imperial Japanese Navy.

The S.E. was in service in America in small numbers after the war. It had been intended to mass produce the type there and a contract for 1,000 was given to Curtiss. The American built S.E.5as were to have Wright-Martin-Hispano-Suiza engines. The Armistice was signed before production was under way and only one all Curtiss built S.E.5a was completed, but fifty six others were assembled from components sent over from England. In Britain the American Expeditionary Force bought thirty eight S.E.5as in October 1918.

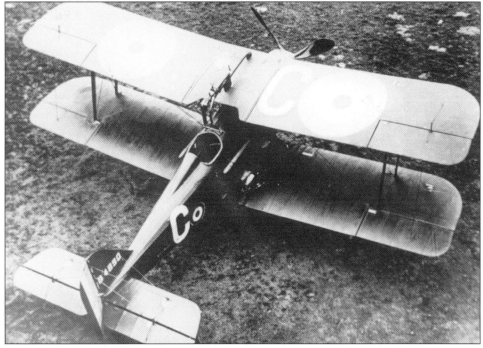

S.E.5a, D4890, of No.56 Squadron, 29 November 1917. Pilot Lt Dodds

S.E.5a with four x 25 lb Cooper bombs under fuselage. Capt. G E H McElroy

A version known as the S.E.5E appeared in America in 1922-23. Fifty were built from spare parts and the suffix letter indicated the name of the constructor, name Eberhardt. The S.E.5E had a plywood covered fuselage and the 180-hp Wright-Hispano E engine.

It was perhaps appropriate that the years of peace should provide no lasting service use for the S.E.5a for it was essentially a machine of war and one of the greatest of its day.

The S.E.5b was an experimental development of the 5a and was built to determine the amount of improvement in performance obtainable by streamlining the engine installation and by fitting sesquiplane wings.

The airframe of S.E.5a, A.8947, was modified to become the S.E.5b. A large diameter spinner was fitted to the airscrew and the engine cowling was neatly and cleanly applied. Instead of the large flat frontal radiator of the S.E.5a a smaller version was installed in the under-slung position. This radiator could be

The cockpit of an S.E.5a

swung backwards and partly retracted. The new wings were on increased area and of unequal span and chord. The interplane struts had a pronounced outwards rake.

It was hoped that the cleaner nose would reduce drag and increase airscrew efficiency. That the larger wing area would reduce the stalling speed and improve climbing characteristics, and that the pilot would have a better all round view than on the S.E.5a.

At low air speeds the S.E.5b proved to be markedly more efficient than the 5a but the larger wings caused enough extra drag to nullify the effect of fairing the nose.

To provide a complete set of comparisons the S.E.5b fuselage was later fitted with standard equal span S.E.5a wings. Ass might be expected this version had a better performance than either the 5a or sesquiplane 5b. In its equal span from the S.E.5b was sometimes known as the S.E.5c. The 5b was also flown without its spinner for the purposes of one series of experiments. At that time the front of the engine was blocked in with a sheet of plywood.

Later the equal span 5b was used in comparative tests with the standard S.E.5a, D.7018, and the S.E.5a, E.5923, which was fitted with a drastically modified tail unit (see S.E.5a history). In these experiments, however,, the S.E.5b had a modified horizontal tail. Its tailplane and elevator had the same total area and planform as those of the standard S.E.5a, but the elevator area was reduced to 35 per cent (from 50) of the total. In this form the S.E.5b was reported to be the best of the three machines and most pleasant to handle

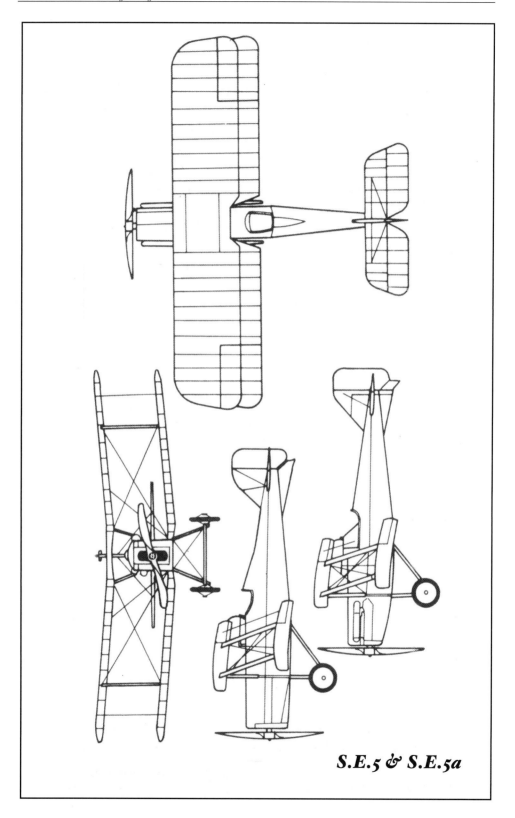

S.E.5 & S.E.5a

CHAPTER THREE

SPAD Fighters

One of the most famous French aircraft manufacturers of the First World War and yet one of the least written about was a company that glorified in the acronym SPAD *(Sociétée pour l'Aviation et ses Derives)*. This came about in the main because of the tight security that surrounded the manufacture of French aircraft during this period. Germany had invaded many parts of France, consequently information about French aircraft was rarely released to the press or anyone else.

The SPAD company had started designing and manufacturing aircraft early in the 1900s, under the control of Armand Deperdussin. In the early days SPAD stood for *Société poure des Appareils Deperdussin*, but in 1913 Armand Deperdussin was arrested and sent to jail on fraud charges. With the existence of the factory hanging in the balance, a syndicate headed by Louis Blériot, took over the company and with it the designer Louis Béchereau. The company retained the name SPAD only this time it stood for *Société pour l'Aviation et ses Derives.*

In the early years of military aircraft manufacturing, one of the problems that faced the designers, was how to fire a fixed machine gun at targets in front of the aircraft, without hitting the propeller. SPAD's chief engineer Louis Béchereau, who had been responsible for the design of the Deperdussin monoplane that won the Gordon Bennett and Schneider Trophy contests in 1913, came up with one of the strangest of designs. It consisted of basically putting a gunners position in front of the engine and propeller. In theory and to a degree in practice it worked, but when it was necessary to work on the engine the gunners nacelle had to be hinged downwards, this made access to the engine area extremely difficult. Nevertheless a number of these two-seat variants were made using this design.

The first of these was the SPAD *SA.1* which was a conventional biplane. The main section of the fuselage was made of wood with four spruce longerons top and bottom with stringers in between. On top of the fuselage and in front of the pilot, were mounted the fuel and oil tanks. The wings were of an unusual design and at the intersection point of the landing and flying wires, there was a two-part articulated auxiliary strut. This enabled a biplane with a large wing span to be braced as a single bay structure, although giving the appearance of a

SPAD SA1.

two-bay structured aircraft.

Powered by a 80-hp Le Rhône engine mounted in the nose, the SPAD *SA.1* had the unusual design of a gunner position mounted in front of the engine and propeller. The 'pulpit' as it was affectionately known, consisted of a framework of ash longerons and covered with plywood. It was supported in the front by two struts attached to the landing gear and by a bearing attached to the rear bulkhead. Two struts attached to the top wing were attached to an 'L' shaped bracket on the aft bulkhead for additional support. The gun, a 7.7mm Lewis machine-gun, was mounted on a vertical track which, in turn, was attached to a semicircular track. This enabled the gunner to both traverse the machine-gun upwards and downwards and to either side.

Communication between the pilot and gunner was a problem, because between them was an extremely noisy engine. In an attempt to overcome this

SPAD SA.2.

problem a tube was connected to the two positions to enable the two men to talk to each other. Not surprisingly the whole system did not prove very satisfactory.

At the beginning of May 1915 the first SPAD *SA.1* took to the air. There were a number of problems with the new aircraft including inadequate engine cooling brought about by the gunner's nacelle in front of the engine, and excessive vibration of the nacelle itself. The variable traversing positions of the gun however received high praise, but even then there was a suggestion that the

SPAD SA.2.

SPAD would be better armed with four fixed machine guns. Only ten of the aircraft were built before an improved version appeared - SPAD *SA.2*. The aircraft was powered a 110-hp Le Rhône 9J engine and the only differences were minor ones. They consisted of changes to the nacelle attachments, the horizontal tail surfaces and the gun mounts.

SPAD SA.2 'MA JEANNIE'.

On 21 May 1915 the first SPAD *SA.2* was flown on its initial test flight. The results prompted the *Aviation Militaire* to order 42 of the aircraft. This was followed by an order from the Imperial Russian Air Service for 57 SPAD *SA.2*s. It is said, that the version sold to Russia was powered by the 80-hp Le Rhône engine and not the 110-hp version that powered the French model.

Rather than place all the SPAD *SA.2*s in one *escadrille* it was decided to assign them to the role of escort fighter amongst the reconnaissance *escadrilles*. From the moment they went into squadron service it became clear that it was not an aircraft that would be welcomed by the crews. Problems were quickly spotted by the gunners, who realised that if the aircraft were to crash on landing, for one reason or another, they would invariably be killed by the engine ploughing through the front nacelle. The pilots also realised that, because of the front nacelle, there was a serious vision problem from the cockpit when landing the SPAD 2 on the rough airfields that served the Allied forces.

In less than a year the number of SPAD *SA.2*s that had been assigned to the various escadrilles had been reduced to four in front-line service and five in training units. Some were lost in combat, whilst others were destroyed in take-off and landing accidents. The development of the SPAD continued however and later that year the SPAD *SA.3* appeared. Only one example of the SPAD *SA.3* was built and consisted of both a front gunner and a rear gunner. The rear

SPAD SA.3 in the factory. Showing the engine and propeller behind the gunner

gunner's position was situated where the pilot sat in SPAD *SA.1* and *2*. Dual controls were installed thus enabling the front gunner to take control of the plane during a rearward attack, but in essence it also meant that the aircraft had to carry two pilot/gunners.

This was obviously not an option so efforts were made to produce another version the SPAD *SA.4*. Using the SPAD *SA.2* airframe and powered by the 80-hp Le Rhône engine, the 110-hp engine was still giving cooling problems, the SPAD *SA.4* appeared. To offset the tail heaviness experienced by the earlier models the wings were repositioned a millimetres further aft. The first flight of the SPAD *SA.4* took place on February 22, 1916 and was reasonably successful. However, only eleven were built – one was taken by the *Aviation Militaire*, the remaining ten by the Imperial Russian Air Service. The reticence in the French military taking the SPAD, was because of the dislike of the aircraft voiced by the aircrews, this was also the case with the Russians but the Russians were limited to what they could buy as far as aircraft were concerned in the early stages of the war. One of the complaints of the aircraft by the Russians, was that the forward gunners position would have a tendency to fall off if the mountings were damaged by gunfire. One report said that a gunner had had his neck broken when his scarf got blown into the propeller and wrapped around the blades.

More than ten percent of the aircraft in the Imperial Russian Air Service during the First World War consisted of SPAD *SA.2* and *4*s. A number of SPAD *SA.2*s were assigned to No.1 Fighter Squadron and the 2nd Guard Air Squadron, whilst the 1st Turkastan Air Squadron of the 11th Division was equipped with two SPAD *SA.2*s and one SPAD *SA.4*.

A diversion from the biplane by Louis Béchereau resulted in the design for a monoplane designated the SPAD *SB*. It was a revolution in design inasmuch as it was intended for mass production. The fuselage was to be moulded from stamped metal to which the landing gear, fuel tanks, wings were all attached. Its role was never announced and never got past the design stage, consequently no details are available.

The SPAD *SC* appeared in August 1915 and had a three-man crew, a gunner in the nose position, a gunner in the rear section of the fuselage with the pilot in between. Powered by a 220-hp Renault engine the performance of this model was far greater than previous models.

SPAD SE - front three-quarter view.

SPAD SE being prepared for a test flight at the factory.

Unfortunately the fighter crews had become disillusioned with the SPAD *SA* series and this was further aggravated by the appearance of the rival Nieuport 11. This fighter exceeded all the expectations and was immediately snapped by the *Aviation Militaire* to fill the gap in the fighter role.

With the fighter market suddenly collapsing around them, the SPAD company turned its attentions to the bomber. The company had submitted a design early in 1915 for a bomber with a four-man crew, two pilots and two gunners. Based on the *SA* series of fighters and powered by a 250-hp Panhard engine, the SPAD *SD* as it was designated, was submitted for the competition for a new bomber but was unsuccessful. Only one was ever built. Undeterred Louis Béchereau submitted another design, the SPAD *SE*, the following year.

Prototype SPAD SG before the guns were fitted in the nacelle

SPAD SG with the three guns fitted in the nacelle.

This time he made a departure from the *SA* series by eliminating the dreaded 'pulpit' gunner's nacelle and installing two 220-hp Renault pusher engines. The aircraft still carried two gunners, one in the nose, the other in the rear and had two pilots seated side by side but in separate cockpits. With a wing span of 24.30m, a length of 13m and a height of 3.45m, this was the biggest aircraft ever designed by Louis Béchereau and built by the SPAD company.

The aircraft was submitted to a competition for a bomber and, together with the Morane-Saulnier *S*, was selected as one of the winners. After a long deliberation, the *Aviation Militaire* decided that they only wanted one bomber and the chose the Morane-Saulnier *S*. Disappointed, Louis Béchereau returned to the designing of fighter aircraft and came up with the SPAD *SF*. This design had a fuselage with two tails and as no design details are available, one can only speculate as to what it looked like. There appears to have been a fuselage with a canard arrangement in the front of the aircraft in which was a gun position, whilst another gun position was situated in the rear fuselage. The pilot's position was almost in the centre of the two fuselages. This is all that is known of the idea and was never brought to fruition. The SPAD *SG* however was, and this was based on the design of the S2 but did not have a gunners nacelle on the front. Instead it was fitted with a fixed Hotchkiss machine gun which was

SPAD S.VII Scout in service with the RFC.

aimed and fired by the pilot. Only one of these aircraft was built and that was only used for testing purposes. Only one other country used the SPAD *S* model and that was Russia, but it was to be a different story with SPAD's next fighter.

After a long deliberation Louis Béchereau decided to move away from the

SPAD S.VII after crashing onto the tennis court in front of the officers mess at Petite Synthe

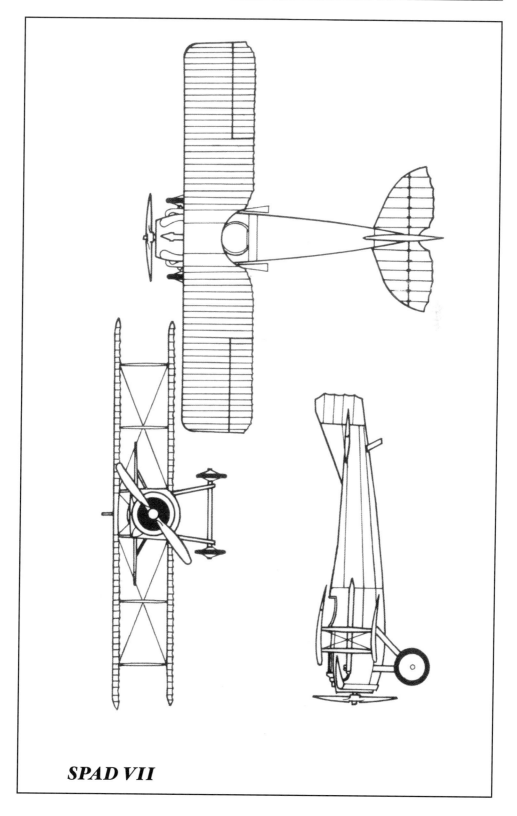

SPAD VII

fighter designs he had created and look toward a new idea incorporating the new 150-hp Hispano-Suiza engine. The Hispano-Suiza engine had been the brainchild of the designer Marc Birigt who had also designed the synchronised mechanism that allowed the 7.7 Vickers machine gun to fir through the propeller blades.

The result was the SPAD VII. The prototype aircraft started life with the designation SPAD V and the first flight took place in July 1916. It was

SPAD S.VIIs preparing for take off.

impressive. It had a top speed of 170 km per hour and could climb to 3,000 metres in 9 minutes. The *Aviation Militaire* had no hesitation in ordering 268 of the aircraft. By the end of September 1916, 24 SPAD VIIs had been delivered and by the end of the year the total delivered had reached 143. Like all new

SPAD S.VII on its tail stand having its canvas fuselage repaired by female members of the RFC.

aircraft there were initial teething problems but nothing too serious. Engine cooling was the biggest problem, or to be more precise, the lack of it. The cowling had to be enlarged together with a system of nine vertical shutters that allowed the pilot to control the amount of air into the engine. The engine bearers had to be reinforced with steel plates after a number of bearer failures caused by excessive engine vibration. The bracing wires had to be modified and the aluminium sockets replaced with steel ones. Surprisingly the was only armed with a single 7.7 mm Vickers machine gun.

To meet the demands of the *Aviation Militaire*, a number of other aircraft

French officer inspecting a SPAD S.VII belonging to SPA 3 Squadron at Maison-Neuve.

manufacturers were brought into build the SPAD VII under licence. They included: SEA *(Société d'Études Aéronautiques)*, Janoir, Grémont, Régy, de Marcay, Mann-Egerton and Blériot *(Aeronautics)* Brooklands. The production lines were now in full flow and by August 1917 495 *SPAD VII* aircraft had been delivered to the *Aviation Militaire* and more than 50 *Escadrilles* were operating the aircraft.

The success of the SPAD drew the attention of a number of foreign military services among them was Great Britain who ordered one which was sent to No. 60 Squadron RFC on 20 September 1916 for evaluation. Pleased with the results, the RFC ordered 30 SPAD VIIs from Blériot (Aeronautics) Brooklands and assigned them to Nos. 30 and 63 Squadrons, RFC, in Mesopotamia, and No.72 Squadron in Palestine. Nos. 19 and 23 Squadrons were the next recipients of the aircraft where, during the Battle of Arras and Messines Ridge, they

SPAD S.VII of the Lafayette Escadrille *flown by Lts. Diddier Masson, Raoul Lufbery and Kenneth Marr.*

carried out numerous ground-attack missions.

The RNAS had also expressed an interest in the SPAD VII and ordered 125, fifty from Mann Egerton and seventy-five from the British Nieuport Company. Although one aircraft was delivered to the RNAS the remainder were re-allocated to the RFC. The RFC ordered an additional 50 SPADs from the French and such was the urgency of the demand, that the French transferred ten from their own *Réserve Générale de l'Aviation*. The remainder were built by the *Avionnerie Kellner et ses Fils* who also took an order for an additional 120 aircraft and spares for 30 more. The order was never fully completed as by July 1917 the French authorities had released a further 30 SPAD VIIs from their reserve stock which was suffice to equip two squadrons of RFC. It was never quite the

Lieutenant Everett Cook, CO of 91st Observation Squadron, USAS, standing beside his personal SPAD XIII, although the squadron itself was equipped with Salmsons.

SPAD S.XIII belonging to Lieutenant Robert Soubiran from the Lafayette Escadrille.

success hoped for with the RFC as a dog fighting aircraft, but for the French and a number of other air forces it proved to be an outstanding aerial weapon.

The United States Air Service were also attracted to the SPAD VII and ordered 167. Many of the aircraft were built by the Mann,Egerton Co. but unfortunately were inferior to those built by the French manufacturers. A number of repairs and modifications had to be made before they would be accepted by the USAS. The 41st. Aero Squadron were the first squadron to receive the SPAD VII at the beginning of 1918, followed by the 138th and 638th

Major Huffers SPAD at the German airfield at Metz after its pilot, Lt. Oscar Gude, USAS, landed there after `running out' of fuel. The Germans dipped the fuel tanks and said that there was ample fuel left in the tanks for the pilot to have returned to his base.

Aero Squadrons toward the end of the year. A number of the aircraft were sent to Kelly Field, Texas at the end of the war to be used as trainers.

The Imperial Russian Air Service were in desperate need of aircraft and by early 1917, the French had sent 43 SPAD VIIs to Russia. So delighted with the aircraft were the Russians, that plans were drawn up to build the aircraft under licence with the *Aktsionyernoye Obshchestovo Dux* plant just outside Moscow. Problems arose soon after production had started with the lack of availability of the Hispano-Suiza engine. The SPAD VIIs that were available were assigned to the No.1 Fighter Group which was composed of four squadrons and were used for escorting bombers on long-range raids. The projected 200 aircraft to be built by the Russian factory was scrapped before the programme could be completed.

After the war the surviving 76 SPADs of all types, *SA 2s*, *SA 4s* and SPAD VIIs, were assigned to various units in military districts, the majority of them being in the Ukraine. They were split between the *Istrebitel'naya Eskadril'ya* in Moscow, the 3rd. *Otryad* of the *Istrebitel'naya Eskadril'ya* at *Kiev*, the 1st. and 3rd. Naval *Istrootryady* at Leningrad and Sevastapol, the 2nd. Naval *Istrootryady* at Odessa, and the School of Military Pilots.

All the SPAD VIIs were assigned to various sections in 1922, four of them to the 4th *Otdek'naya Istrebite'naya Aviaeskadril'ya* at Minsk, four to the *2nd. Otdel'nyi Istrebitel'nyi Aviaotryad* at Kharkov, three to the *1st. Morskoi Istrebitel'nyi Vozdukhchast* and the remainder sent to the 1st. Higher School of Military Pilots and the Training *Eskadrill'ya*. In 1925 all the SPAD aircraft were withdrawn from service. Two the Russian SPAD VII aircraft however were captured by the Ukranians and saw service in the Ukranian Air Service until 1920.

Among the other European countries that acquired the SPAD VII, were Belgium who in September ordered 15 to replace their aging Nieuport 17s and placed them with the 5th Escadrille. An additional seven were ordered and delivered six months later. Even Finland managed to obtain one, albeit one that was captured in 1918. It did remain in service with the Finnish Air Force until 1923. Holland also obtained a SPAD VII under similar circumstances when they interned one of the aircraft after it had landed on Dutch territory. The Dutch purchased the aircraft from the French with the intention of building the aircraft under licence, but none were ever built. Estonia purchased two SPAD VIIs in 1925 and were used in the Estonian Air Service.

Italy was one of the countries that acquired a number of SPAD VIIs, in fact their entire air force consisted mainly of French built aircraft. Surprisingly the Italian pilots did not rate the SPAD VII as high as their Nieuport 17s or Hanriot HD.1s as a fighter aircraft. As a high-speed reconnaissance aircraft however it was regarded very highly. Although a number of SPAD VIIs were

Georges Guynemer's SPAD `VIEUX CHARLES at Dunkirk.

allocated to nearly all the *Gruppos*, they were soon relegated to training and reconnaissance units and replaced with Hanriot HD.1s. This came about because the SPAD had to be obtained from France, whilst the Hanriot HD.1 was being built under licence by the Italian aircraft manufacturer Macchi.

The Polish Air Force acquired a number of SPAD VIIs at the end of 1917 and equipped their newly formed 1st. Polish Combat Aviation Unit with them. A second unit, the 2nd. Polish Combat Unit was formed at the beginning of 1918 and given one SPAD VII, but before it could be put into operation, the base at Kanev where the aircraft was based was overrun by the Germans. The units reformed and an additional 15 SPA VIIs supplied. Another country, Serbia, had a number of SPAD VIIs serving alongside their Nieuport 17 fighters. Based at Vertekop with the 1st. and 2nd. Serbian Escadrilles, which made up the 1st. Pursuit Group, they carried a number of attacks on the retreating German army.

During the war in the east, Greece purchased 16 SPAD VIIs and equipped their 531 Squadron with the aircraft. Together with a number of Nieuport 24bis fighters, the SPADs were based at Gorgupi, where they stayed until the end of the war.

The Czechoslovakian Air Force purchased 50 SPAD VIIs and XIIIs after the war and assigned to various flying schools. In 1924 they were withdrawn from service and replaced with a mixture of Russian and homegrown aircraft. Even Romania purchased 8 SPAD VIIs at the end of the war together with several SPAD XIIIs and put them into *Grupi 3 at Galatai.*

Spain had intended to build the SPAD VII under licence after Colonel Rodriguez Mourelo had negotiated an agreement with the French manufacturers. The firm of Pujol, Comabella & Cia were selected to build the aircraft after Captain Eduardo Barrón had overseen the adaptation of the French design. Only one of the aircraft was ever built. It was plagued with

SPAD S.XIII.

numerous defects to such an extent that the *Servicio de Aeronautica Militar* dropped the whole project and negotiated with the British Martinsyde company to build the Martinsyde F.4 under licence.

Three Portuguese pilots served with SPA 124, also known as the *Lafayette Escadrille*, during the First World War and had flown a number of aircraft including the SPAD VII. After the war the Portuguese Air Service purchased 12 SPAD VIIs for the purpose of developing their own air force. They were assigned to the *Grupo Independente de Aviacao de Caca*, later the unit was reinforced with 4 Martinsyde F.4 Buzzards three years later. The unit became the *Grupo Independente de Aviacao de Proteccao e Combate* in 1927 and five years later the SPAD VIIs were withdrawn from service.

Outside of Europe Argentina purchased two SPAD VIIs and two SPAD XIIIs, assigning them to operate with *Grupo de Aviacion 1*. *Peru* even purchased two SPAD VIIs after they had been demonstrated by a French Military Mission. Both aircraft were based at the *Centro de Aviacion Militar* at Maranaga as trainers. The Chilean Air Service purchased one SPAD VII in 1918 in an effort to develop their own air force.

The Japanese Air Service purchased three SPAD VIIs in 1918, with the intention of building them under licence as they had down with the Henry Farman and Curtiss aircraft, but the agreement never materialised.

Even the far eastern country of Siam purchased two SPAD VIIs for their air service.

The SPAD VII, although only a single-seat fighter armed with a single 7.7mm Vickers machine gun, it laid out the groundwork for the SPAD XIII C.I. A total of 3,500 SPAD VIIs of all variants were built, the aircraft acquitting itself with almost every Allied air force in the First World War.

In August 1917 came the arrival of the SPAD XIII. Initially powered by a 220-hp Hispano-Suiza 8BA engine, but later by the Hispano-Suiza 235-hp 8BEc engine, the aircraft was eagerly accepted and rapidly replaced the Nieuport 28 and SPAD VII in virtually all the Escadrilles. It was armed with twin Vickers machine-guns in place of the single Vickers machine-gun in the SPAD VII. The SPAD could climb faster than any of the British fighters and although extremely manoeuvrable in combat, was a very tricky to handle at low speed. Unlike the S.E.5A which could literally float down on landing, the SPAD XIII had to land with full power on. It could also dive faster than any other aircraft of the time, Allied or German, such was the robustness of its construction.

The *SPAD XIII* was of a box-section construction, the fuselage consisting of four spruce longerons with spruce struts and cross-members. They were braced with heavy gauge piano wire which were pulled tight and made off on wiring plates attached to the joints. The engine bearers, unlike those of other aircraft, extended in to the cockpit to support the pilot's seat.

The upper wing was made in a one piece structure with hollow box sections whilst the ribs were made of plywood, the whole structure was then covered in linen and doped. The leading edges of the wings were made of spruce, whilst the trailing edges were made of wire. The main interplane struts were made of duraluminium tubing.

The SPAD XIII was in action with a number of the French aces, including René Fonck who ended the war with a tally of 75 `kills'. Amongst those `kills' was one quite remarkable incident that happened on 9 May 1918 whilst on a morning patrol over the Somme. He encountered a German two-seat reconnaissance aircraft being escorted by two Albatros fighters. Within just a matter of minutes Fonck had dispatched the three of them. That same evening whilst on patrol he encountered another two-seat reconnaissance aircraft with its Fokker D.VII fighter escort. After a brief skirmish he shot down the three aircraft raising his tally to six for the one days patrol.

Georges Guynemer was flying one of the first SPAD XIIIs assigned to an escadrille, when he disappeared after dogfight over Poelcapelle, Flanders.

The aircraft was assigned to the United States Army Air Service and made up nearly all of the aircraft in their inventory. The reason for this, was that the Americans had no military aircraft of their own and had to be supplied from the Allies inventory. A number of the American pilots had seen service with the French *Escadrilles* since the beginning of the war, including the famous *Lafayette Escadrille*. As the final year of the war progressed, the influx of American troops and aircrews into the Western Theatre of the war was the killer blow to the Germans and their allies. A number of American pilots came to the fore during this period, Eddie Rickenbacker, Frank Luke and Raoul Lufbery to name but a few all of which flew the SPAD XIII for most of their service.

Such was the robustness of the SPAD XIII that the aircraft was still in service with the French Air Force until 1923 and a number of them were sold to Japan, Italy and Belgium. It was without question one of France's most successful aircraft of the First World War

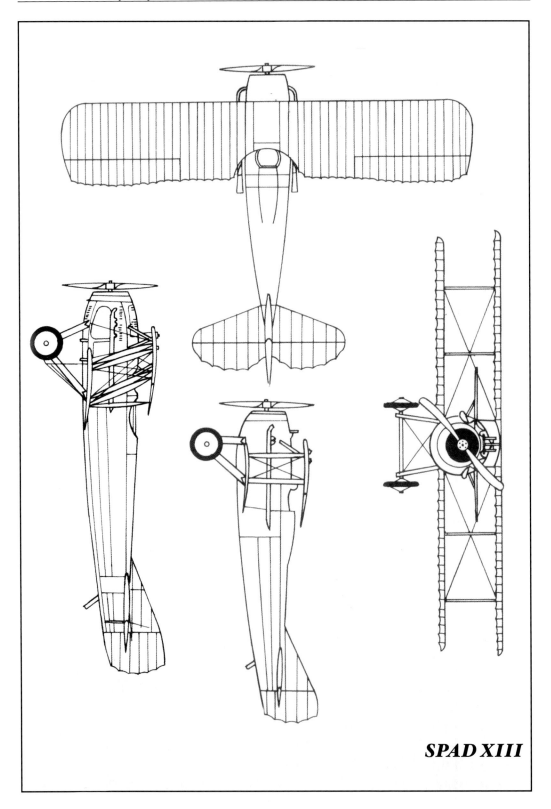

SPAD XIII

CHAPTER FOUR

Siemens Schuckert D Series

It was big, bulky and could have been considered the Thunderbolt of the First World War, and it was German. From the front and plan view if was a purposeful looking fighter and pleasing to the eye but, when seeing the elevation, the whole design was flawed in that the fin and rudder assembly was ugly even though functional. However, the fighter's saving grace were the colour schemes given them by the *Jastas* that flew them. The blazing scarlets, deep blues and chocolate schemes enhanced the fighter's appearance, and many of the pilots went further with their personal adopted emblems and painted sections.

Development of this magnificent fighter started in the summer of 1916 when the *Siemens Schuckert Werke* built three airframes with which to flight test the bulky, new 160-hp. eleven cylinder air cooled rotary engine.

The company was founded in 1847 as *Siemens Halke* and changed to *Siemens Schuckert* several years later when it merged with another company. The new company concentrated on telegraphic equipment and it was not until 1907 that it established an aviation department at the request of the German General Staff to design and build a non-rigid airship.

Having established the new department the company decided to design

Siemens-Schuckert D.I. The appearance of the aircraft look as if it has just come out of the factory.

aeroplanes and in the early 1900s it produced three monoplanes which were soon rejected. As a result the company closed its new department but when in August 1914 the German Air Force required a steady flow of new designs of aircraft the company reinstated it under the directions of Dr. Walter Reichel.

Its first products were the so called 'giants', large bombers for the purpose of bombing England and France from the homeland, and a number of them were considered to be successful, although they were built in small numbers.

The company's efforts were then directed to the production of fighters with the result that a small batch of monoplanes of the Taube type were designed and built as prototypes. Inevitably these were also rejected. It was now 1916 and although the company had produced several sub-contracted types its design staff were ordered to design and construct new biplane types.

Their first attempt was almost a 'Chinese copy' of the French Nieuport 17, and was an excellent design although showing much similarity to the French product. However, the German Air Staff accepted the new biplane and placed an order for 150 D.1s and it went into production in 1916. Production of the specified engine, the Siemens Halske, however, was beset with problems and consequential delays that led to the cancellation of a second order for 100 examples.

By the time it was ready for service trials events had overtaken it and the aircraft never made much of an impression.

However, like the British S.E.5, a new engine was to breathe life into an idea for a larger type of biplane to be powered by the new, experimental, Siemens Halske engine, a radical design having eleven cylinders rotating around the camshaft which was stationary. It had a 1,200/1,500 rpm range but what made the engine different was that the crankshaft rotated in one direction at 900rpm and the cylinders in the opposite direction.

The design improved propeller efficiency and its only fault, which was serious, was it ran at a high temperature. but the effect of the slow rotation of the engine meant that it did not require the complication of reduction gearing. The total horse power produced was 160, high for that period of time and Siemens Schuckert designers decided to produce a fighter around it.

Leading the design team was Harald Wolff and both he and his assistants quickly produced large biplane fighter in the April of 1917 for which a contract was placed for three prototype airframes under the designation of D.II, (serial number D 3501/16), D.IIa, (D 3500/16) and D.IIb, (D 3502/16), for the sole purpose of test flying the new S-H engine.

As with a large number of both German and Allied engines teething troubles soon plagued the new engine and it was not until late summer did the first example reach the Siemens Schuckert works. In appearance the three

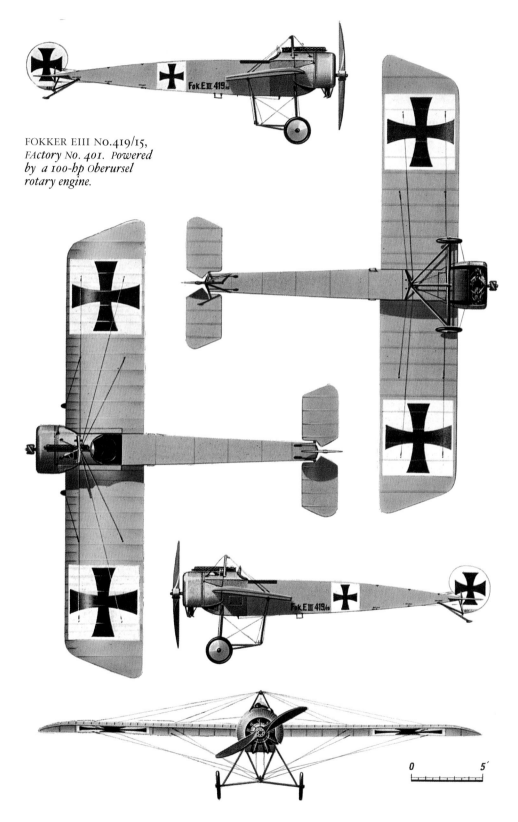

FOKKER EIII No.419/15,
FActory No. 401. Powered
by a 100-hp Oberursel
rotary engine.

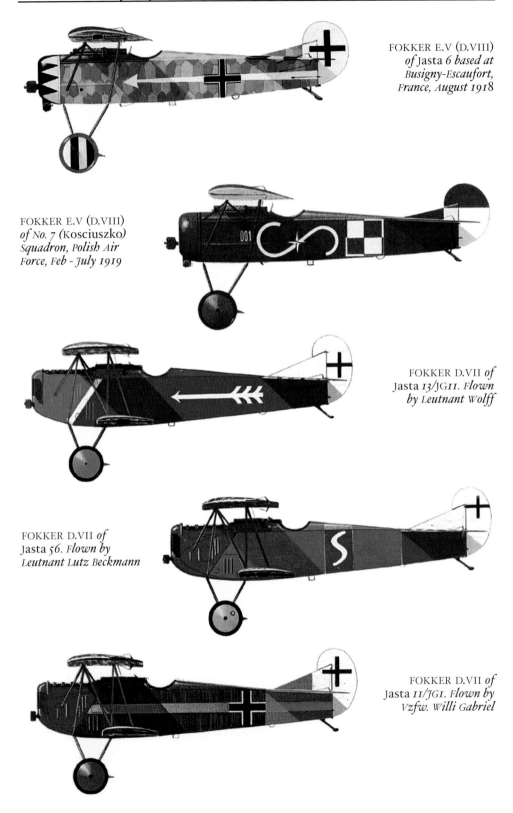

FOKKER E.V (D.VIII)
of Jasta 6 *based at
Busigny-Escaufort,
France, August 1918*

FOKKER E.V (D.VIII)
*of No. 7 (Kosciuszko)
Squadron, Polish Air
Force, Feb - July 1919*

FOKKER D.VII *of*
Jasta 13/JGII. *Flown
by Leutnant Wolff*

FOKKER D.VII *of*
Jasta 56. *Flown by
Leutnant Lutz Beckmann*

FOKKER D.VII *of*
Jasta 11/JGI. *Flown by
Vzfw. Willi Gabriel*

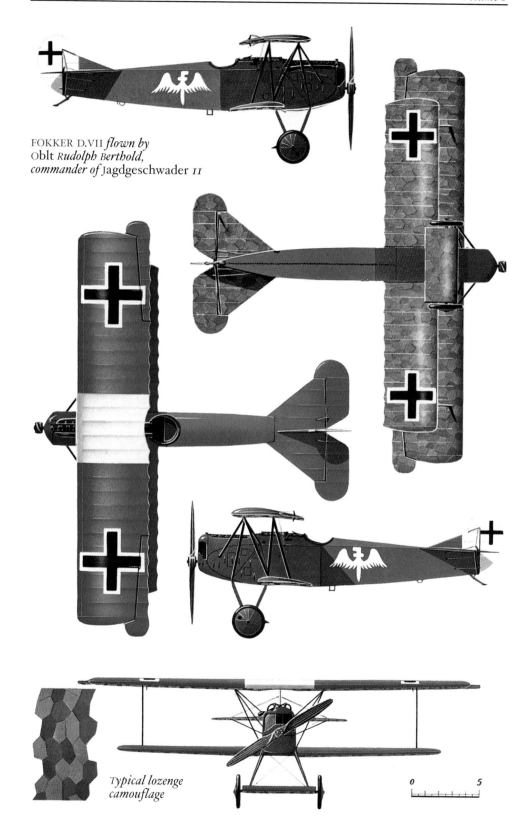

FOKKER D.VII *flown by* Oblt *Rudolph Berthold, commander of* Jagdgeschwader *II*

Typical lozenge camouflage

0   5

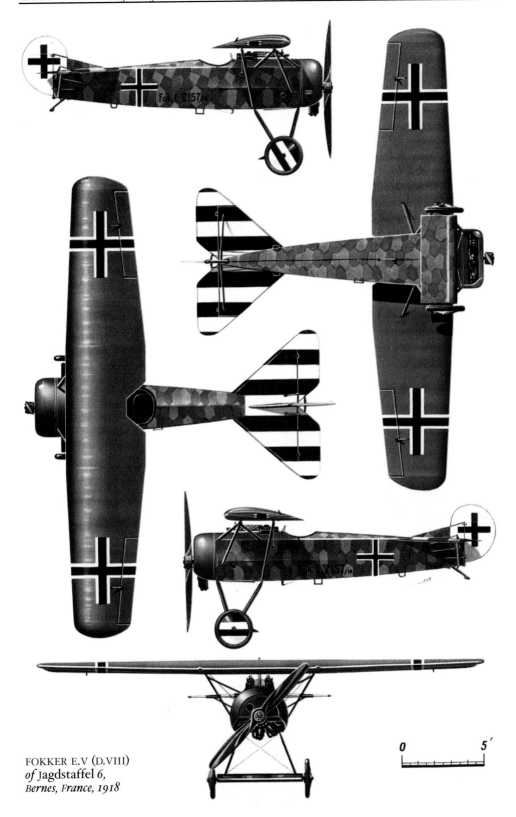

FOKKER E.V (D.VIII)
of Jagdstaffel 6,
Bernes, France, 1918

0   5′

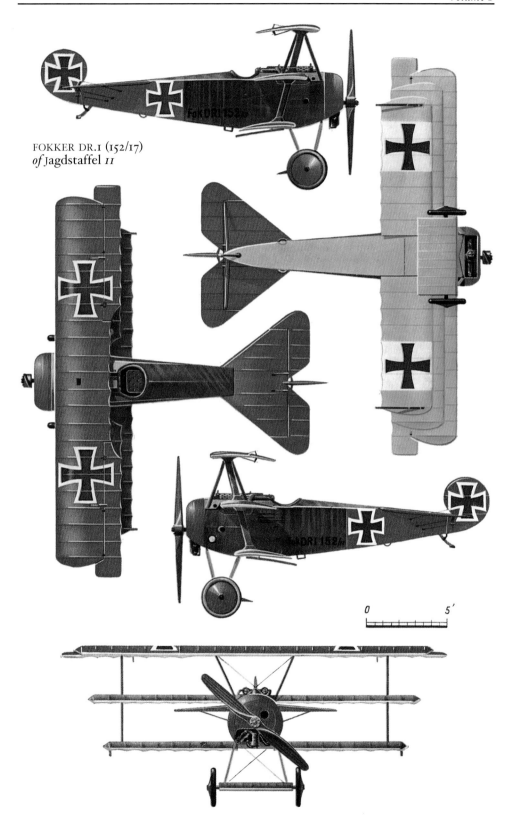

FOKKER DR.I (152/17)
of Jagdstaffel 11

0   5′

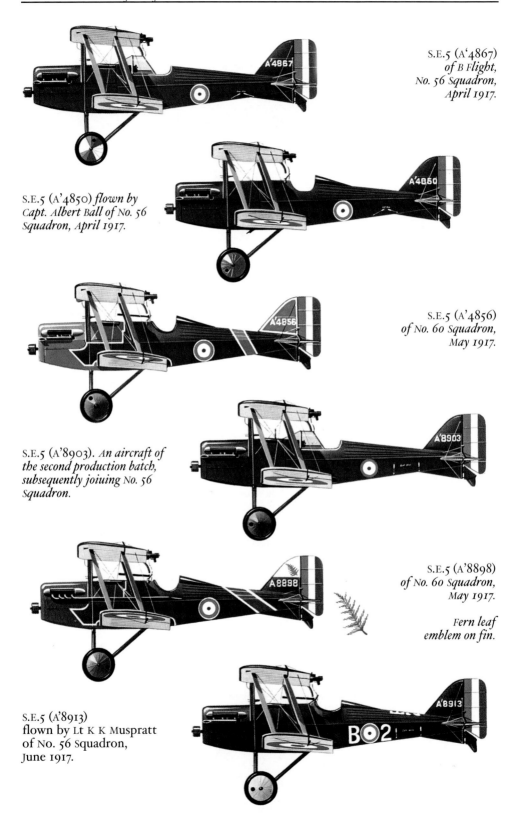

S.E.5 (A'4867)
*of B Flight,
No. 56 Squadron,
April 1917.*

S.E.5 (A'4850) *flown by
Capt. Albert Ball of No. 56
Squadron, April 1917.*

S.E.5 (A'4856)
*of No. 60 Squadron,
May 1917.*

S.E.5 (A'8903). *An aircraft of
the second production batch,
subsequently joiuing No. 56
Squadron.*

S.E.5 (A'8898)
*of No. 60 Squadron,
May 1917.*

*Fern leaf
emblem on fin.*

S.E.5 (A'8913)
flown by Lt K K Muspratt
of No. 56 Squadron,
June 1917.

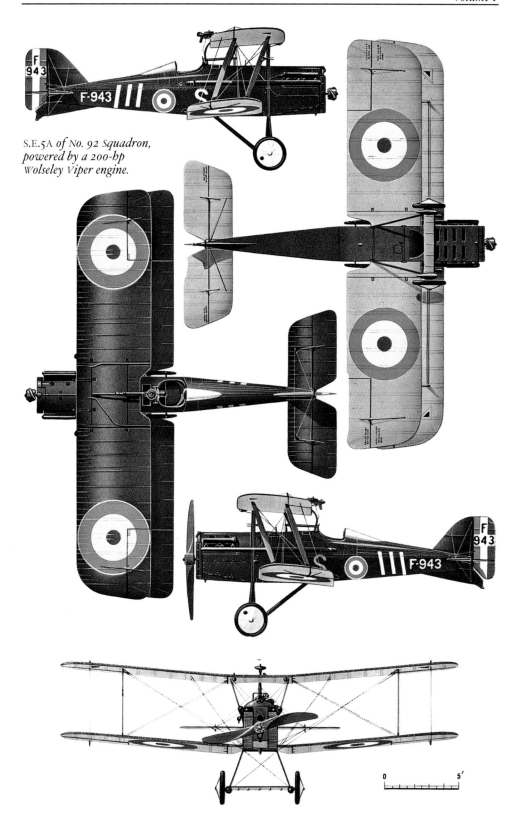

S.E.5A of No. 92 Squadron, powered by a 200-hp Wolseley Viper engine.

SPAD XIII CI *of the 22nd Aero squadron,* A.E.F.

camouflage of lower wings.

Insignia of the 22nd Aero Squadron.

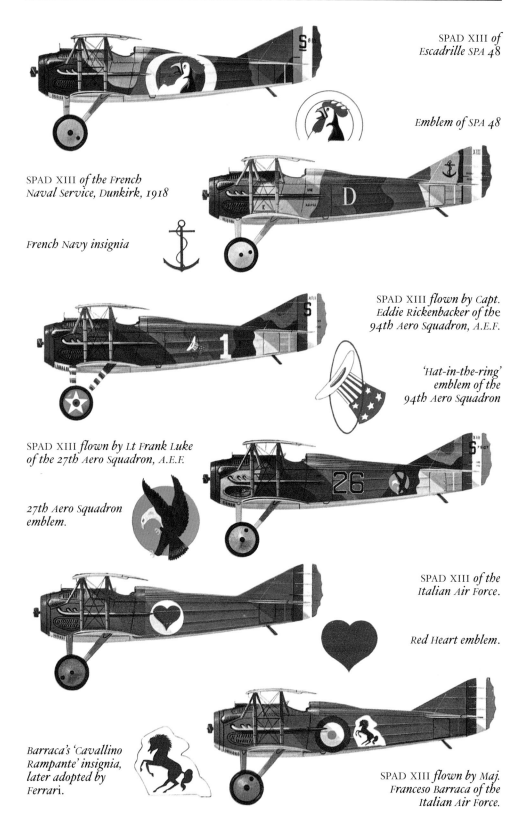

SPAD XIII *of*
Escadrille SPA *48*

Emblem of SPA *48*

SPAD XIII *of the French*
Naval Service, Dunkirk, 1918

French Navy insignia

SPAD XIII *flown by Capt.*
Eddie Rickenbacker of the
94th Aero Squadron, A.E.F.

'Hat-in-the-ring'
emblem of the
94th Aero Squadron

SPAD XIII *flown by Lt Frank Luke*
of the 27th Aero Squadron, A.E.F.

27th Aero Squadron
emblem.

SPAD XIII *of the*
Italian Air Force.

Red Heart emblem.

Barraca's 'Cavallino
Rampante' insignia,
later adopted by
Ferrari.

SPAD XIII *flown by Maj.*
Franceso Barraca of the
Italian Air Force.

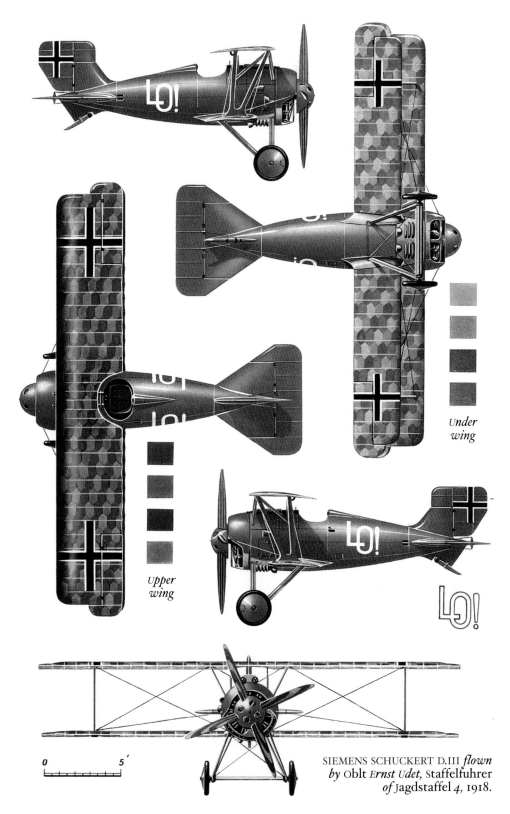

Under wing

Upper wing

0   5′

SIEMENS SCHUCKERT D.III *flown by* Oblt *Ernst Udet*, Staffelfuhrer *of* Jagdstaffel 4, 1918.

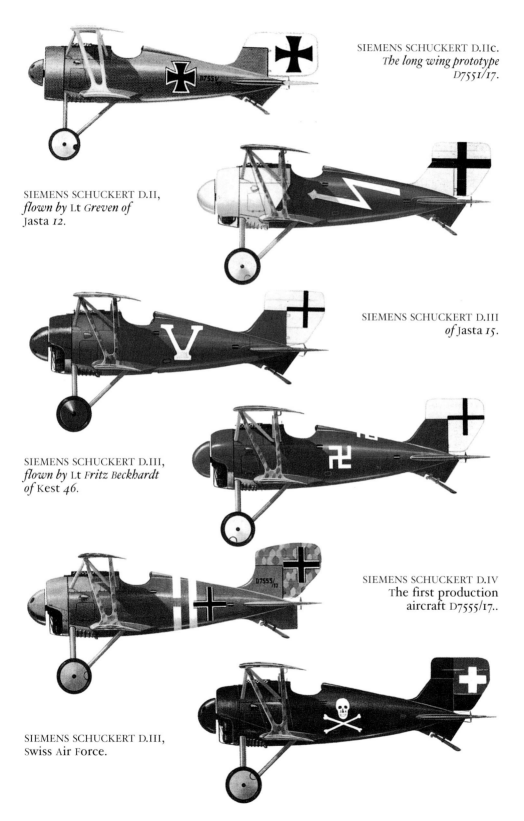

SIEMENS SCHUCKERT D.IIc.
The long wing prototype
D7551/17.

SIEMENS SCHUCKERT D.II,
flown by Lt *Greven of*
Jasta *12.*

SIEMENS SCHUCKERT D.III
of Jasta *15.*

SIEMENS SCHUCKERT D.III,
flown by Lt *Fritz Beckhardt*
of Kest *46.*

SIEMENS SCHUCKERT D.IV
The first production
aircraft D7555/17..

SIEMENS SCHUCKERT D.III,
Swiss Air Force.

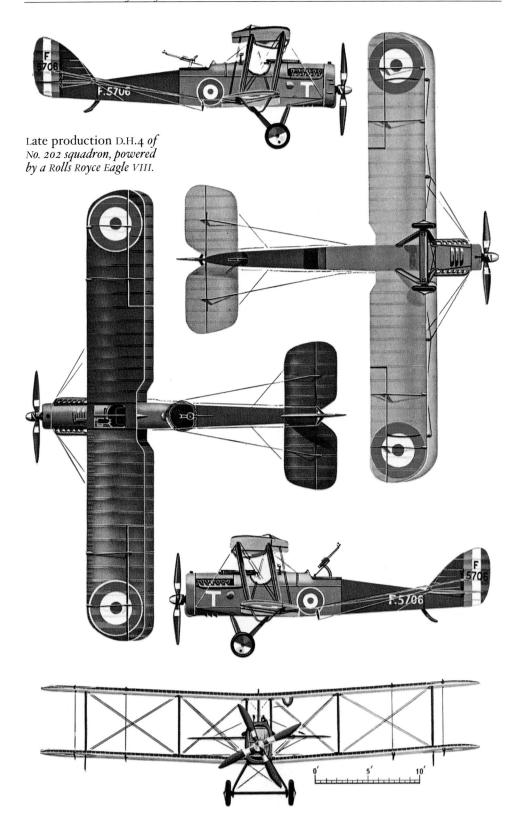

Late production D.H.4 *of
No. 202 squadron, powered
by a Rolls Royce Eagle VIII.*

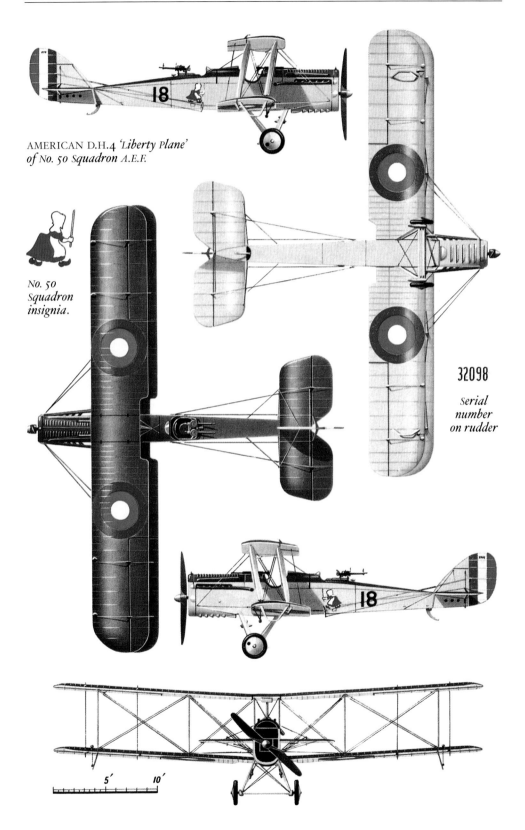

AMERICAN D.H.4 *'Liberty Plane'*
of No. 50 Squadron A.E.F.

*No. 50
Squadron
insignia.*

32098

*Serial
number
on rudder*

5′ 10′

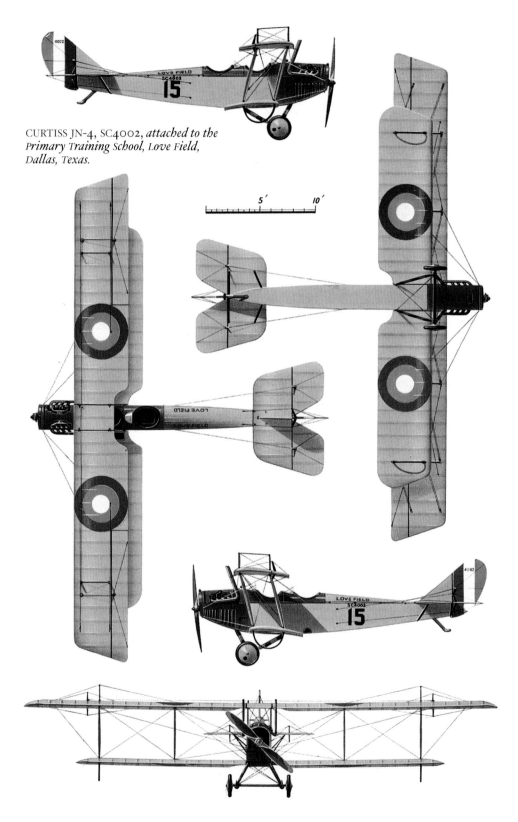

CURTISS JN-4, SC4002, *attached to the Primary Training School, Love Field, Dallas, Texas.*

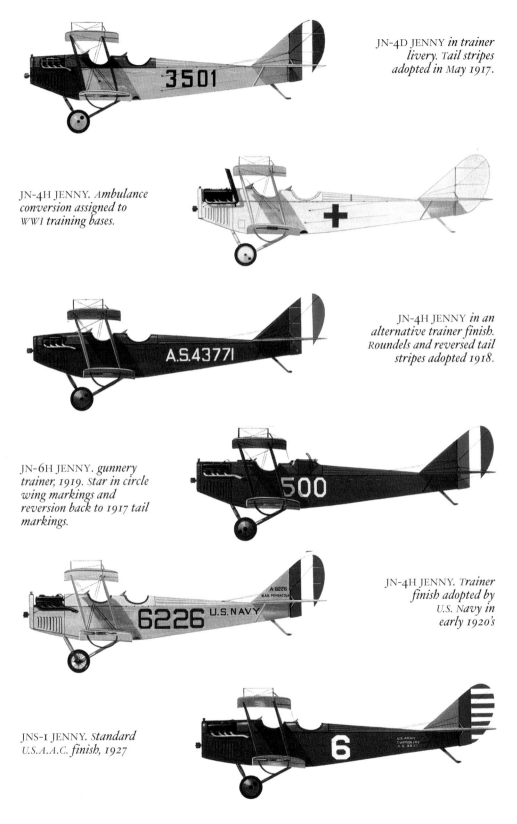

JN-4D JENNY *in trainer livery. Tail stripes adopted in May 1917.*

JN-4H JENNY. *Ambulance conversion assigned to WWI training bases.*

JN-4H JENNY *in an alternative trainer finish. Roundels and reversed tail stripes adopted 1918.*

JN-6H JENNY. *gunnery trainer, 1919. Star in circle wing markings and reversion back to 1917 tail markings.*

JN-4H JENNY. *Trainer finish adopted by U.S. Navy in early 1920's*

JNS-1 JENNY. *Standard U.S.A.A.C. finish, 1927*

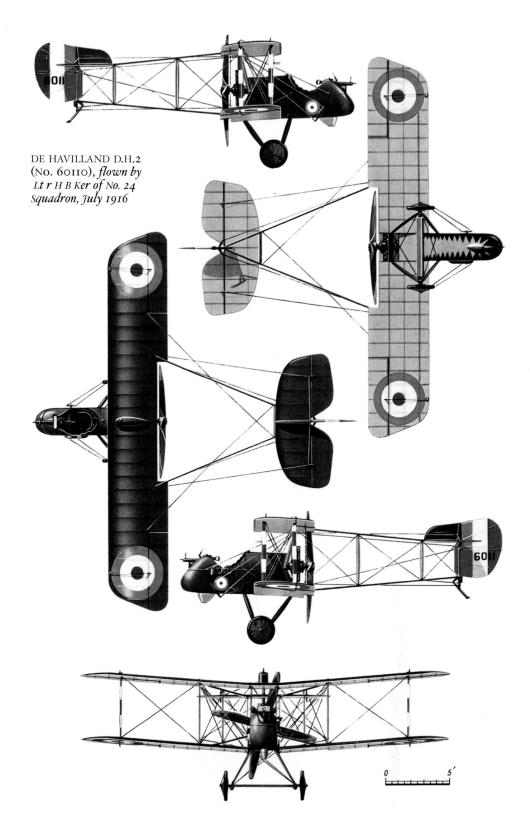

DE HAVILLAND D.H.2
(No. 60110), *flown by
Lt r H B Ker of No. 24
Squadron, July 1916*

prototypes had a large, bulky airframe and a short moment arm giving them a stocky look.

The test programme produced some results that promised a sound future for the design and the D.IIb reached a height of 16,500ft in just fifteen minutes and then went on to establish a height of almost 23,000ft in 36 minutes. Satisfied

Siemens-Schuckert E.I monoplane

with the results the German Staff ordered three additional machines as the D.IIc short, (D 7550/17 *kurz*), D.IIc long, (D 7551/17 *lang*), and D.IIe, (D 7553/17).

The order was subject to an improvement in level speed, which was being equalled by aircraft already in service. They went into a second test programme under the new designation of D.III, and more satisfied with the results of the

Siemens-Schuckert D.III on its tail stand.

trials an order was placed for twenty production machines. In the opening months of February 1918 a second order for thirty aircraft was placed and they were ready just in time to take part in the great German offensive of that year.

Although all the prototype aircraft had been built to the same specification and design, the D.IIc short had a modified wing arrangement with reduced chord on the upper wing. The airframe was eventually modified as the first production prototype D.IV. The D.IIe long (7553/17) had metal wing spars in order to test fly in without the inter-wing bracing cables. However, subsequent trials established that the wings flexed considerably leading to the cables being re-introduced. In the event the aircraft was finally rebuilt to D.IV production standards and was sent to *Jagdgeschwader* II in April/May 1918 for service

Siemens-Schuckert D.III with the spinner removed.

evaluation. It was returned to the Siemens Schuckert factory for experiments and modification before being returned to the German Air Service as an operational machine.

Deliveries of the first production batch of D.IIIs were made to the Air Service in January 1918 and all had four bladed wooden propellers. Alongside production aircraft a third batch of development aircraft were being produced as six machines, three D.IVs and three D.Vs, the latter having two bay wings.

It was *Jagdgeschwader* II that was again selected to conduct operational trials on the Western Front in April 1918, flying with *Jasta 12* and *16* and an immediate fault was revealed. The Siemens Halke engines were now enclosed in large cowlings and they over heated and on occasions seized-up completely, this being the result of insufficient trials in an endeavour to get aircraft and engine

Siemens-Schuckert D.III fitted with its spinner.

into service.

As a result all operational D.IIIs were returned to the S-W factory in early summer 1918 for various airframe modifications and new, and improved, engines. The modifications and new engines were immediately incorporated into the third batch (30 aircraft) of fighters on the production lines and the most obvious modification was the cutaway lower section of the engine cowling in order to induce additional cooling. Despite all this effort the subsequent production aircraft were used for homeland defence.

The D.IV Design.

A new young designer, Heinrich Kann, had been engaged to work on improving the design. He immediately set to work to produce a completely new wing design, which consisted mainly of reduced area of both upper and lower wings of identical design with a chord of approximately three feet. Initial flight trials revealed and improvement in speed over that of the D.III of 118mph plus a better climb of 16 minutes to a height of 19,500 feet.

A production order was immediately placed in late March 1918 but due to production difficulties sufficient numbers did not reach the squadrons until August that year with deliveries to *Jastas* 14 and 22. The *Marine Luft Feld Jasta* was also supplied with a small number of aircraft. Additional supplies were available the following September but by then the great German push and faltered and stalled as the Allied forces held the advance and went over to the final offensive of the war with newly arrived American troops. All in all the *Jasta* had a trickle of the D.IV, insufficient in numbers to make any real improvement

Siemens-Schuckert D.IV showing the bottom half of the engine cowling cut away

in the air war. Although it is thought that a total production run of 280 aircraft was reached no more that twenty percent ever reached the *Jastas*.

However, although few machines did see service in the German Air Force they were considered superior even to the new Fokker types. *Jasta 22* had a small number of D.IVs and the flying personnel considered it was the best biplane fighter on the Western Front including the Bristol Fighter and S.E.5a. During one sortie a D.IV climbed to 19,000 feet in less than fifteen minutes with a full war load. Despite this praise, however, its maximum performance was restricted

Remains of a Siemens-Schuckert D.IIID of Kest 5. The cypher on the side could be that of Prince Frederick of Prussia.

to fairly short periods due to engine problems such as over heating. Another fault was ground looping and over-turning due to the relative fast landing speeds. Despite its fairly radical design the D.IV followed standard engineering practices with its fuselage of circular section built up on four main longerons

Siemens-Schuckert D.IV of Jagdegeschwader *1 on its tail stand.*

with transverse bulkheads all connected by diagonal formers upon which was glued and pinned a three plywood covering, virtually an early form of semi-monocoque assembly. At the front end was the geared rotary engine mounted on a spider mount which later had the bottom segment cut away to the centre line to improve engine cooling. A large hemispherical spinner enclosed the propeller which was of a coarse pitch. This spinner had to have four louvers between the blade roots to guide air on to the crankcase.

The fin and tailplane were an integral part of the rear fuselage with the same plywood covering, and the fin had an asymmetrical section, which counteracted the enormous engine torque. The rudder was hung on hinges and horn balanced. In shape the tailplane was an arrowhead and the one-piece elevator was fabric covered on steel ribs. The rudder was also fabric covered.

The wings of the D.III and IV were the same basic shape and based upon two box spars which were spindled out from root to tip to a fixed thickness except at the strut and compression member locations where they were solid. The wing ribs were of 1.5mm three ply with pine cap strips and were secured by wooden blocks glued into position.

The upper wing was a one-piece structure and had overhung, steel tube, horn balanced ailerons located at all the four wing tips. The lower wings were built in town panels and attached to the lover fuselage. The centre section struts were of an 'N' form as many of the time and attached to the upper wing longerons. The lower wings were attached to the struts by securing points on the longerons.

The interplane 'V' struts were structured from spruce hollowed to reduce weight and fabric wrapped for strength. The whole wing cellule was diagonally brace with steel cables with a drag wire running from engine cowling to the lower interplane strut junction. As an added aid to counteract torque the D.IV cellule on the port (left) side was four inches longer.

The 'V' strut undercarriage was a conventional structure with main circular steel tubes and faired with aluminium. A steel spreader bar was fitted behind the rear struts to hold the whole unit together. A diagonal cable was braced in the plane of the rear struts. The axle was secured to the struts by steel coil-spring shock-absorbers. An ash tail-skin was secured to an integralky built play triangular underfin.

Leading particulars

Wing span: (D.III) 27ft.8in. (D.IV) 27ft 4.75in.
Area: (D.III) 203.5sq.ft. (D.IV) 163.25 sq.ft..
Length: (D.III/D.IV) 18ft.8.5in.
Height: (D.III) 9ft.2in (D.IV) 8ft.11in.
Weights: tare (D.III) 1174 lbs, gross 1595 lbs. (D.IV) tare 1190 lbs, gross 1620 lbs.
Max speed: (D.III) 112.5mph. (D.IV) 118.75mph.
Ceiling: (D.III) 26,575ft. Climb to 6,575ft. in 3.75min, to 9480ft in six mins, to 13,100ft in 9mins, to 16,00ft in 13mins and to 19,680 ft in 20mins.
Ceiling: (D.IV) 26,250ft. Climb to 3280 ft in 1.75min.
Duration: two hours.
Engine: Siemens Halske Sh III of 160hp and Sh IIIa of 200hp. Later Sh IIIa of 240hp.
Armament: two x synchronised Spandua machine guns firing through propeller disc.

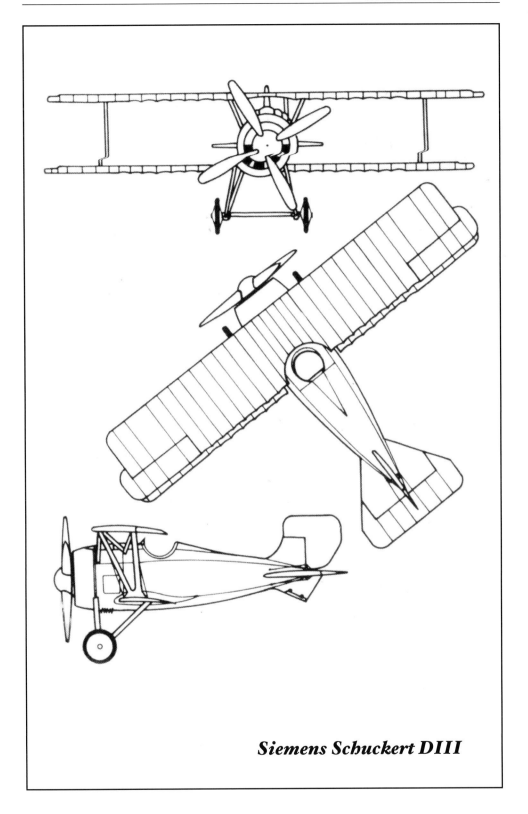

Siemens Schuckert DIII

CHAPTER FIVE

The Airco D.H.4

Until the appearance of Geoffrey de Havilland's D.H.4 single-engine bomber, the R.F.C. (Royal Flying Corps) had to struggle to carry out any bombing attack with adaptations of the single-seat Scout aircraft. The D.H.4 can, therefore, claim to be the first design dedicated to the task of carrying out bombing raids against an enemy target, and yet contemporary journals of the period referred to it as the 'First, really high-speed British General Utility machine', of medium weight fitted with a high-powered engine.

It was also de Havilland's first tractor biplane (pulled by the propeller rather than pushed) he designed while employed at the Aircraft Manufacturing Co., (Airco) of Hendon, a suburb of West London. He had always maintained that

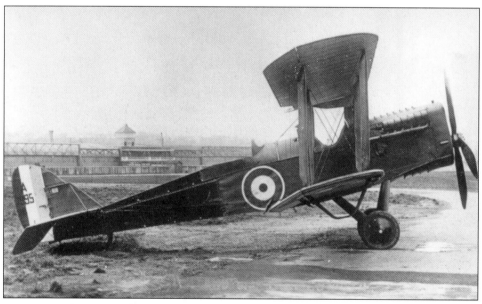

Airco/ de Havilland D.H.4 bomber variant

the tractor aeroplane was more efficient than the pusher, of which de Havilland had designed two (D.H.1 and D.H.2) for Airco, although the latter were more suitable for a forward-firing machine-gun without having to fire through a whirling propeller.

The appearance of the Fokker E.1, which had such a weapon system, persuaded British designers of the suitability of the interrupter gear and to quickly resolve the problem as the German fighter was wreaking havoc among

R.F.C. aircraft. Eventually, after a number of designs were tested, the new Constantinesco hydraulic synchronised gear proved the most successful and de Havilland decided to use it for his new tractor bomber, the D.H.4.

This design was a two-seat bomber in which the pilot was the bomb-aimer and in charge of the forward-firing Vickers machine-gun mounted on the upper fuselage. The observer/air gunner, in a second seat, was armed with a Scarff ring-mounted single or twin Lewis. The bomb load was, normally, two x 230 or four 112 lb missiles.

In the D.H.4 the R.F.C now had one of the great aircraft that fought in the First World War. The basic design was typical of the period with a conventional, box girder structure in two sections, the forward section of which was plywood covered, the aft with fabric. The wing had two spruce spars spindled out between the compression ribs and balance cables. These interconnected the upper ailerons of the upper wings. The tailplane was built of wood and fitted with a

D.H.4 'A1' and Sopwith B.1 (N50), of No.5 Squadron, Petite Synthe, 1917.

variable incident gear with the fin and rudder assembly taking on the profile that became de Havilland's hallmark. To enhance communication between pilot and observer there was a speaking tube leading from one cockpit to the other.

Reports of trials by the National Physical Laboratory stated that the aerodynamics of the new bomber were unequalled at that time, and its use in various roles, even when up against singl- seat Scouts, helped re-establish Allied control of the air in 1916.

To appreciate the significance of the D.H.4 to the R.F.C. and Air Board it was specified that the Beardmore 160-hp engine be fitted as standard and that the aircraft be designed around it. The water-cooled, six-cylinder in-line engine had been designed by a young engineer, F.B.(Frank) Halford, who had modified a standard 120-hp Beardmore engine. So impressed were Sir William Beardmore and T.C.Pullinger, the original manufacturers, that they backed Halford in producing a new more powerful (200-hp) engine that became the Beardmore-Halford-Pullinger or B.H.P.

Pilot climbs into the cockpit of his D.H.4 of No. 5(N) Squadron.

The B.H.P. was similar to the original Beardmore in being a six-cylinder, in-line engine with a cast aluminium monobloc with steel liners. This choice was influenced by the superb Hispano-Suiza design of the period. The first engine was subjected to bench running in June 1916, following which it was installed in the prototype D.H.4, serial 3696, instead of the 160-hp Beardmore.

It was not until this new prototype airframe and engine flew from Hendon for the first time in August that some difficulties were apparent with the new engine. It was necessarily modified before it was declared suitable for series

D.H.4, serial N6000 'B1' of No.5 (N) squadron, Petite Synthe, Dunkirk, late 1917.

production and it was not until July 1917, that the first batch of engines were ready for delivery to Airco. Fitting the modified engine a major fault was discovered in the airframe as the engine mountings had been designed using data of the early B.H.P. engine. This, and the fact that B.H.P. were not able to produce the engine in great quantity, caused de Havilland to look elsewhere for an engine to power his new aircraft.

An alternative was available as the Rolls-Royce Company was developing a new, liquid-cooled 'V' engine of 250-hp which became known as the Eagle. Although priority for this engine had been applied to installations in the Admiralty's large floatplanes, after bench running trials had been successfully

Line of D.H.4s powered by RAF 3a engine. Note Swastika on one aircraft.

concluded from a start in May 1915, production versions were leaving the factories from the end of October 1915.

By the time the first production D.H.4s were ready for engine installation sufficient quantities of the Eagle were available and these, and the limited numbers of the B.H.P, were installed. Fortunately, sufficient production models of the D.H 4. were ready for delivery to No. 55 Squadron, R.F.C. before the unit left for France on March 6, 1917.

Subsequently the airframes were being completed in greater quantity than the supply of engines from the B.H.P. and Rolls-Royce factories. Alternatives were installed including the 200-hp R.A.F. 3a, a 'V' unit with a single, central exhaust stack and a four blade propeller; the Siddeley Puma of 230-hp (a variant of the B.H.P) and the 260-hp Fiat.

The Fiat powered machine had an upright engine and the exhaust and upper cylinders stood proud of the cowling inhibiting the pilot's forward view. . There was also a D.H.4 Renault 12Fe powered variant of 300-hp. Pilots were cautioned

D.H.4A civil passenger type built by de Havilland.

against lifting the tail too high during take-off as the propeller could strike the ground. When more powerful engines, such as the R-R Eagle VIII, were installed in the D.H.4 the undercarriage height was increased to allow for a larger propeller that was necessary with the increased horse-power.

Satisfied with their new bomber the Air Board placed orders with Airco, and sub-contractors for 1700 D.H.4s. The Royal Navy Air Service operated the new bomber which was built by Westland with part of the order for 150 being powered by the R-R Eagle and incorporating two forward-firing Vickers machine-guns and one in the rear cockpit for the observer. However, this

Possibly the same aeroplane as above. F5764, ex-G-EAWH.

weight increase drastically affected the overall speed of the aircraft. One of the aircraft for the R.N.A.S. had twin floats installed as an experiment. There was no tail float but, following trials at Martlesham, a number were fitted with floatation gear or hydrovanes and tip floats. The undercarriage was jettisoned before ditching.

Two examples, including A2168, were evaluated for use as a COW (Coventry Ordnance Works) quick firing gun bomber/Zeppelin destroyer. The weight of the shell was 1.5 lb. and the gun was installed to fire upwards at a fixed angle with the breech almost touching the fuselage floor. The muzzle protruded

Airco-built D.H.4, F4746.

through the upper centre section which was covered with metal because of the blast. The pilot sighted the gun and the gunner fired it. Early production models had the Scarff ring mounted on the top fuselage longerons, but these were below the upper decking and prevented effective operations of the guns. Later models were modified by raising the gun-ring to the upper fuselage.

Engine development during the war advanced at a rapid pace and suitable flying testbeds were required. The D.H.4 was a natural choice and the engines tested were the 300-hp. Renault F3 in A2148, the 400-hp Sunbeam Mayabele (A8083), and the 353-hp Rolls-Royce G. One had an R.A.F.3a engine installed and additional, long range fuel tanks to raise endurance to almost 14 hours. Camouflaged in matt Fawn and Blue they were for reconnaissance duties. The first target was to be the Keil Canal but the Admiralty cancelled the sortie and the two aircraft were diverted for anti-Zeppelin duty. The Ricardo-Halford supercharger, which due to its height hindered the pilot's view, was re-designed

Crowd of pilots and observers collecting their American-built D.H.4, summer of 1918.

as an inverted installation.

In the United States the Secretaries of the War and Navy Departments were presented with a procurement programme of 7375 aircraft to be powered by the Liberty engine before it had been completely developed. Both Departments wanted to test the new 400-hp Liberty 12 in the D.H.4 as they had already made plans to build it with an initial requirement of 1700. One aeroplane, without an engine, was sent from Airco to McCook Field on August 15, 1917 and it made a first flight with the 400-hp engine on October 29, 1918.

The D.H.4 came up to American expectations and production contracts were placed with the Daytown-Wright, Fisher Body and Standard Aircraft

D.H.4 with two bladed propeller.

Company for a total of 9500 examples. The first completed aeroplane was delivered by Dayton Wright in February 1918, and joined the American Expeditionary Force (A.E.F.) in France on May 11, 1919. A total of 3227 Liberty powered D.H.4s were built in America before the Armistice was signed. Batches totalling 1885 had joined twelve squadrons with the A.E.F. in France by November 1919.

At the war's end 7500 American D.H.4s were cancelled but many were successfully converted to D.H.4B standards (up to a total of 1538) by many contractors. Two hundred and eighty-five D.H.4 and 4Bs had steel tube fuselages made by Atlantic and Boeing and these became the D.H.4M. Large numbers

Winner of the 1922 first King's Cup race was F L Barnard in G-EAMU

were used for mail carriers and passenger liners with several hundreds being sold to the civil market for various purposes. A racing version was the D.H.4R, with clipped wings and a 450-hp Napier Lion engine, which went on to win the 1919 Aerial Derby. Another example had an experimental Rolls-Royce engine, the Model G of 353-hp @ 1800rpm.

The Russian Air Force purchased the D.H.4 and the engine selected was the Fiat. In anticipation of delivery a hundred Russian pilots were in training, and fifty aircraft were being built in Russia. The R.F.C. deliveries were running behind schedule and after talks with the Russian government an agreement was reached that fifty of the aircraft scheduled for Russia were to be diverted. In exchange the Russian Air Force would receive 75 D.H.4s in the spring of 1918. Many other countries used the de Havilland machine including Greece, Spain.

D.H.4, N6000 of 5(N) squadron, 1917/18, Flt Cdr C P O Bartlett.

The D.H.4 in Action.

The first operational sorties of the new bomber were by No. 55 Squadron on April 6, 1917, when a flight of six attacked the railway station at Valenciennes and, a few weeks later in May, they bombed the Busigny railway junction. Reconnaissance sorties were also flown by No. 57 Squadron who took delivery

Pilot C P O Bartlett in his D.H.4 with Col. Dugdale. N5974.

of its D.H.4s in May 1917 in time for the Battle of Ypres (Wipers as it was known to the British Tommy). Nos. 18, 25, 27 and 49 followed and fought in the Battle of Cambrai along with the new tank battalions. Two PR(Photo Reconnaissance) squadrons were formed with the D.H.4, Nos. 25 and 49.

All the D.H.4s bombed from 14,000 to 16,000 ft, but they were thrown into a ground attack role in early 1918 to help stem the retreat from the advancing

D.H.4, A7624 of No.55 Squadron.

Germany Armies. In October 1917 the D.H.4 joined the VIII Brigade, which became the Independent Force, R.A.F., to begin strategic bombing against Germany. They were to take part in 95 operations on major German cities including Cologne and Frankfurt.

The R.N.A.S. (Royal Naval Air Service) began accepting deliveries of the D.H.4 in spring 1917 and were used for day bombing, coastal patrol and reconnaissance. The first deliveries went to No. 2 Naval Squadron at St Pol while the Sopwith 1 1/2 Strutters of No. 5 Naval Squadron were also replaced by the D.H.4. During anti-submarine patrol duties No.217 Squadron, flying the D.H.4, had two direct bomb hits on the U.B.12 in August 1918. The Navy also operated the aircraft for anti-Zeppelin patrols

Royal Navy Units operated with the D.H.4 in the Balkans and Middle East, as did Italian based examples, and R.A.F Squadrons were transferred to Russia.

Uncle Sam's D.H.4s

If ever a country was not capable of launching an attack by air it must have been the United States of America in April 1917. The sinking of American shipping by the German U-boat fleet convinced the American Government that Germany, apparently, considered any ship, whether neutral or Allied, to be a legitimate target.

The Army Air Force was in a pitiful state with the Aviation Section of the Signal Corps without a single, combat-worthy aeroplane. The American Government was of the opinion that due to the huge industrial base of the nation, this situation would soon be resolved with mass production of the necessary aircraft.

However, this was an error of judgement as the aircraft needed had to be designed first, then developed and finally assigned to a variety of roles. For this situation to be realised not one, but numerous types of aircraft were required – land based bombers, ground attack, reconnaissance, transport for coastal patrol/anti-submarine, which was best carried out with long range, large seaplane boats. The list was long and complicated, and American industry was

Liberty-engined American D.H.4s

geared to civilian markets – the production of motorcars, road and rail transport and a myriad of domestic goods.

A study of that period reveals how the American Government threw money into the industry in a desperate attempt to retrieve the situation. Military Purchasing Missions were sent to Europe to examine, evaluate and order aircraft that would be delivered to American Forces in Europe, until the time the American aviation companies could design and produce aircraft that were as advanced as those in operation by the opposing forces in Europe.

A glaring example of the bad judgement of the Purchasing Missions was the Italian based Mission that purchased complete aeroplanes, such as the multi-engined bombers as supplied to the Italian Air Force. These aircraft were hardly capable of lifting their own weight into the air without further encumbering them with any military load. The large Caproni bombers are a good example. for when the Purchasing Mission placed large orders for Caproni's giant bombers, the Italian industry demanded total control of production.

The American Government, concerned about such a situation, wanted to preserve production of major components for their own aviation industry. The idea was, initially, to allow the companies to manufactured and learn about European production aircraft and then to build all major components in America for shipment to Italy and final completion, after which they would be delivered to French and Italian squadrons.

U.S.-built D.H.4 powered by American-built Liberty engine.

Insofar as the British multi-engined bombers were concerned only two companies and two designs, the Handley Page 200/400s and Vickers Vimy, were on offer, and these were acceptable to America as they would be built by their own industry.

The de Havilland/Airco D.H.4 also fitted the category of production in and by American factories and labour force, for delivery to the A.E.F. from the homeland. The Allies collaborated to a certain degree, each anxious to protect their own industries but their concerns were understandable. America's industrial power was capable of producing the requirements of the whole of the Allied Air Forces, and that would leave the Europeans without any worthwhile aviation industry.

However, compromise is all and, in the case of the D.H.4, America and

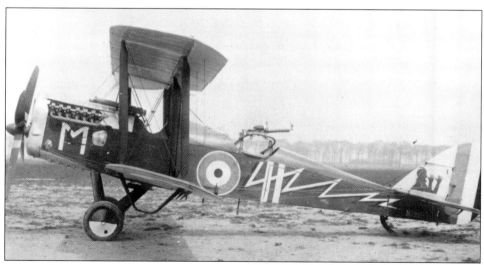

D.H.4 of No.202 Squadron. Note the derisory tail emblem.

Britain were comfortable with the position of building and developing the de Havilland light bomber. The aircraft was also to be powered by an American engine, the very new Liberty 12 of 395 to 400-hp, even though it was still in the design stage.

The French were more pragmatic and although that Government supplied a number of A.E.F. squadrons with the Nieuport and SPAD fighters, they also asked America for the supply of 8000 aircraft to be delivered before May 1, 1918. In terms of history the United States had only twelve months to prepare for a war from scratch with little knowledge of mass aircraft and engine production. Also, the French wanted reserves and trainers in support to a total of 20,000. It was a mad scheme, particularly so when the American automobile industry virtually dictated the fledgling aircraft industry with minimum consultation, leaving the latter with very little to contribute. Companies like the Fisher Body Company, a division of the General Motor Group, dominated manufacturing of imported designs to be built under licence. These designs, initially for fighters, were the Bristol Fighter, one of the very best of the war era, S.E.5 and SPAD XIII and, of course, the D.H.4.

The staggering sum of $617M was allocated and spent, and when compared to the numbers of fighters that reached the French battle areas, the sum per aeroplane that saw action was enormous.

America Adapts the D.H.4

As related above the first British D.H.4 to arrive in America was delivered, without an engine on July 27, 1917, and was transferred to McCook Field, Dayton, Ohio, H.Q. of the Technical Staff Aviation Section on 15 August. The first

American pilots and ground crew members. 278th Observation Squadron.

Liberty engine was bench tested on the 25th. By the following October the first engine to be produced was of 395-hp and, on the 29th, it made its first flight in the D.H.4.

Such was the faith in the engine and airframe that a Procurement Programme for the combination had been presented to the Secretaries of War and Navy Departments for 7375 aircraft. All appeared well for the Liberty powered D.H.4 but engine design and development had been rushed and problems soon arose. The core of the problem rested with the problems associated with (1) a new, and virtually untried engine (2) building a suitable factory and (3) tooling and assembly of mass produced aircraft/engines. American industry had never encountered such a huge industrial problem before. Motorcar design and subsequent production could be phased in to a given plan that evolved as the production and development progressed over several months, but not so for the aircraft industry.

With the D.H4 and Liberty engine thousands of engineering changes had to be made from the obvious conversion from the Imperial to American measurement standards down to the change of screw threads already established by the Society of Automotive Engineers. The Liberty engine was a Government sponsored design that was to be manufactured by chosen contractors under the direction of the U.S. Army, which controlled all production and supplied the Navy and Marines.

The de Havilland basic construction was not altered and the fuselage continued to be built in three separate sections. The cockpit and engine section retained its use of wooden longerons and plywood covers. The fuselage, from cockpit to tail was a fabric covered wooden frame with wire bracing and a plywood covered tail assembly. Wings were of standard routed wooden spars and a thin R.A.F.15 section of ribs manufactured from wood and glued to strips.

Wing bracing was initially of American, round stranded wire, soon to be replaced with streamlined R.A.F wires. The undercarriage was a built up laminated 'V' attached together by straight, horizontal spreader bars. A floating axle was secured by bound rubber chord.

Despite the obvious advantage of having a production and war service fighter/light bomber available without the delay of original design and development, there was considerable opposition to the American D.H.4, even though the A.E.F. had no contemporary American design. However, the automotive industry had been put into action and could not be delayed. Too much was at risk. It was recognised that the design was nearing obsolescence and the Airco Company had produced the de Havilland D.H.9. In the event that latter design was found to be almost on par with its predecessor.

It was a delicate situation. The A.E.F had no equipment and the other

Aircraft 'B5' comes to grief. Note twin Lews guns in rear cockpit.

designs from France would not be available for mass production until evaluated. A number of Nieuports were provided but they were not as good as the British machine. American designers, and aircraft manufacturers, were confident of producing aircraft of equal, and on some instances, bette standardsr, but the Army held the purse strings and controlled contracts and believed that what mattered was instant production.

When these restrictions were removed it was too late to remedy the situation. The Liberty Plane as the D.H.4 was known was an accepted fact, in large scale production and the Air Service was committed to use it for the foreseeable future.

Like the British version contact between pilot and observer/gunner was by means of a speaking tube as their cockpits were separated by the main fuel tanks. In the heat of battle there was no time to plan tactics and crew members had to act on their own initiative. In a crash the pilot's life was often in jeopardy. The undercarriage was also providing its own problems. It was situated too far

Major T Bowen and companions of the 1st Day Bombardment Group.

aft, upsetting the Centre of Gravity and making the aircraft nose heavy. Large numbers were to land, or taxi, only to tip forwards on to the propeller, with subsequent damage.

Brave, or foolhardy, rear occupants were often seen sitting astride the rear fuselage during the landing procedure and preventing a nose over. Aircraft were known to catch fire even when not fighting an enemy. As was usual in both World War aircraft the D.H.4 joined the ranks of `Flying Coffins'.

Armament of the American D.H.4 was superior to that of the British version with two x .303 in calibre Marlin or Browning machine-guns firing forward, and two x .303in Lewis guns mounted on a Scarff ring in the rear cockpit. Underwing racks held a maximum of 12 any mix of bombs to a total of 322 lbs.

Personnel of the First Aero Squadron.

Other equipment was cameras wireless and night-time flares.

Through hard work and inspiration all the D.H.4s quirks were eliminated when the D.H.4B (American) appeared, but too late for war action. The first American produced D.H.4 reached France on May 11, 1918 when the German advance was rolling up the Allied front lines. They had to be assembled and flight tested, guns fired and aligned and the usual pre-operation measures completed. The first to see action was on August 2 with a total of twelve in readiness. By the following November it was all over and just twelve squadrons of the A.E.F were ready for combat, and that included the bomber version. The Combined Navy-Marine Northern Bombing Group had four D.H.4 squadrons covering the Belgium coast. The A.E.F managed to deploy just 196 at the Front

(Zone of Advance) out of a total 696 available from a total of 1213 delivered.

There were a great many D.H.4s available at the time of the Armistice of November 1918, and with the D.H.4B model in production in America, they were considered only for scrap. In a wasteful exercise they were stripped of all salvageable military equipment, piled up in a huge mound and burned. The cost of dismantling, crating for shipping, landing or stored for re-assembly was greater than the value of the stripped airframe, an excellent example of over production in the way of a newer model.

The American D.H.4B

The first American variant was the 4A with a modified fuel system, but the first major change of configuration was in the 4B. Crew seating was changed with the fuel tank forward of the pilot allowing direct communication with the observer/gunner. The undercarriage was moved forward to improve landing and the whole fuselage was strengthened with plywood covering. Thanks to the D.H.4 the American aircraft industry was supported by contracts for converting surplus stocks into the Model 4B, thus giving an impetus to the aviation industry although, in the longer term, it was only Boeing that survived the Great Recession of the 1930s.

After the war the Army took the opportunity to adopt a letter-number system for new aircraft while the older, wartime models retained theirs. These were-

DH.4B-1	with 110 gals main fuel tank plus an eight gals reserve.
DH-4B-2	had the 76 gal. leak-proof main tank plus the normal eight reserve.
DH-4B-3,	135 gals main fuel tank and reserve.
DH-4B-4	Civil passenger version with 4B-1s fuel capacity.
DH-4B-5	carried two passengers in cabin behind pilot. 4B-1 fuel capacity.
DH-4BD	Department of Agriculture crop duster experimental.
DH-4BG	with chemical smoke under-wing containers.
DH-4BK	equipped with specialised gear for night flying.
DH-4BM	mail and courier type with rear passenger seat and baggage compartment.
DH-4BM-1	Dual control version based on the 4BM. Fuel capacity, 135 gals. Built by Boeing.
DH-4BM-2	transport version based on 4BM-1.
DH-4BP	Photo reconnaissance with cockpit cameras.
DH-4BP-1	standard PR version.
DH-4BP-2	experimental aircraft with D.H.9 wings and 135gal tank.
DH-4BP-3	similar to 4BP-1 with 100gals tank.

XDH-4BS   supercharged Liberty engine and 88 gal. tank.

DH-4BT   two seat, dual control trainer.

DH-4BW.   A total of 4Bs powered by 300hp. Wright-Hispano H engine.

DH-4C   350-hp. Packard 1A-1237 engine test-bed.

XDH-4L   racing version of nine hour endurance.

DH-4L   revised, slim, fuselage civil type with 185 gals tank.

The above list is of official designations, and in addition there were many more including those experimental variants used by the Air Service Test Centre at McCook Field. The DH-4Ms were rather specialised variants developed by a number of the companies that had modification contracts. Boeing Airplane Company was conducting experiments with steel tubing for the main, load bearing, structures. In 1923 they had an Army contract for the 180 new Boeing Model 16 known as the DH-4M (modernised). The first three prototypes were designated as XDH-4M. Thirty percent of the Boeings were transferred, by order of the Navy, to the Marine Corps. The 02B-1 with Marine Corps equipment; 02B-2, four built, were for passenger carriage. The DH-4M1 was the rebuilt 4M with further, modern modifications; the DH-4M-1K target towing variant. DH-4M-1K dual control trainer as was the 4M-1T. DH-4M-2K target tug. DH4-M-2P Photo-Reconnaissance. DH-4M-2S with supercharged engine. DH-4M-2T dual control trainer. DH-4Amb-1 ambulance for single stretcher. DH-4AMB-2 for two stretchers

As late as 1924 Boeing modernised the 4M by installing tapered wings. The Air Service had three known as the XCO-7, Experimental Corps Observation, Model 7. Two had the Liberty upright engine with the third fitted with the inverted model. An Army modification was the XCO-8 with Loening COA-1 wings installed on an Atlantic built DH-4M2. The Model 42 XCO-7 Series produced also a static test model, the -7A was a DM-4M-1 fuselage and Liberty engine and other modifications, while the -7B had balanced elevators and the inverted Liberty. These aircraft were flight tested at McCook Field.

Leading particulars of XCO-7A. Observation Model

Wing span: 45ft.0in, area: 440sq.ft. Length; 29ft.2in. Height; 20ft.8in. Weights; tare; 3107 lbs, gross; 4665. Max speed; 122mph, cruise; 110. Ceiling: 13,050ft, climb @ S/L 810ft/min. Range: 420 miles. Engine: Liberty 21A of 420hp. Fuel as above. Armament: four x .30in m/gns.

U.S. Government mail contracts were flown by the surplus Curtiss `Jenny' and D.H.4. These were modified, normally, with the forward cockpit faired over to produce a 500 lb. mail compartment. They also had large, powerful landing lights at wing tips. The L.W.F Company modified the majority and produced its own variant which was a twin engined conversion with two, 200-hp Hall-

Scotts. Ten were built for the Army and 20 for the Post Office. A number had the Loening wing modification.

American Camouflage Markings

The first American 'Liberty Planes' were a Creamy White upper wing surfaces scheme and a Khaki-Brown fuselage that extended half way down the sides. This colour was also used for the tailplane. The scheme was changed in late 1918 to a Khaki-Brown overall. In 1926 all Army aircraft, including the DH-4s, had bright Yellow wings and tail surfaces.

The Navy 4s also had the Cream-White scheme but this was changed to the Yellow wing and tail surfaces and the remainder in Silver. National markings were a roundel of Red outer, Blue middle and White centre. A number carried the White Star marks./ Tail stripes in Red, White and Blue were adopted in 1918 and Red on the rudder leading edge.

In 1926 the Army changed the rudder stripe to a single Blue vertical with 13 alternating Red and White stripes. The Navy and Marines retained the three strips arrangement. Post-war Boeing 4Ms were Olive Drab overall until 1926 when the Yellow wing uppers were adopted. Navy models were Yellow uppers and Silver unders.

View of crowded cockpit of D.H.4. RFC/RAF version of the RNAS configuration.

Variants (does not include American 4s)

D.H.4. Two prototypes plus 1449 production examples built by Airco and main sub-contractors.

D.H.4A. Liberty engine variant for two passengers in rear cabin. Operated No.2 (Communication) Squadron between England and Paris during Peace Conference. Fitted Triplex windows and hinged (upward) roof. With Aircraft Transport and Travel, four new aircraft. Many surplus aircraft converted by Handley Page for H.P.Transport Ltd. Buenos Aires for River Plate Aviation.

D.H.4R. Single racing aircraft with 450-hp Napier Lion engine and shorter span wings.

DH-4. U.S. built aircraft. See above.

Service Use

R.F.C. Squadrons in France. Nos. 18, 25, 27, 29, 49, 55, 57, 97, 98. **R.N.A.S.** Nos. 2, 5, 6, 11, 17. **R.A.F** Nos. 205, 206, 211.

Overseas. Nos. 30, 63, 72, 220, 221, 222, 223, 224, 225, 226, 227. **Various.** No. 10, 51, 110 Training.

A.E.F. France. 8th, 11th, 20th, 85th, 96th, 100th, 135th, 155th, 166th, 168th, 278th, 354th.

Sub-contractors home and abroad. The Aircraft Manfacturing Co, F.W.Berwick & Co; Palladium Autocars Ltd; Vulcan Motor and Engineering Co; Waring and Gillow Ltd; Westland Aircraft; Atlantic Aircraft Corps; Boeing Airplane Company; Daytown-Wright Airplane Co; Fisher Body Corps; Standard Aircraft Corps.

Engines installed. R.A.F3a (200-hp); B.H.P (230); Siddeley Puma (230); Rolls-Royce Mk.III (250); Rolls-Royce Mk.IV (250); Fiat (260); Rolls-Royce Eagle VI (275); Renault 12Fe (300); Wright H (300); Packard 1A-1116 (300); Packard 1A-1237 (300); Armstrong Siddeley Jaguar I (320); Rolls-Royce Eagle VII (325); Rolls-Royce G (353); Rolls-Royce Eagle VIII (375); Ricadro-Halford supercharged; Liberty 12 (400); Sunbeam Matabele (400); Liberty V-1410 (420); Liberty 12A (435); Curtiss D-12 (435); Packard 2A-1500 (525).

Leading particulars of 1916 Airco D.H.4

Wing span: 42 ft 4 in., area:.434.sq. ft, .gap: 5 ft. 6.in., chord: 5 ft 6 in.

Length: 30 ft 0 in. Height: 11 ft 4.5 in. Tailspan: 14 ft 0 in., area: 81.1 sq ft. Rudder area: 13.7 sq. ft. Fin: 5.4 sq. ft. Max speed @ S/L 120 mph, landing: 52 mph. With R-R engine 136.5 mph. Climb to 6500 ft in 8 mins, to 10,000 in 14.10 mins, to 15,000 in 29.15 mins. With R-R engine to 15,000 ft in 16.30 mins.Weights, tare 2302 lbs, military load of 578 lbs, gross 3400. Wing loading 7.84 lb.sq.ft, power 14.35 lb/hp. Engine: B.H.P of 240-hp. Propeller diameter 8.75, pitch 8.2, rpm 1355. Fuel 66gals.

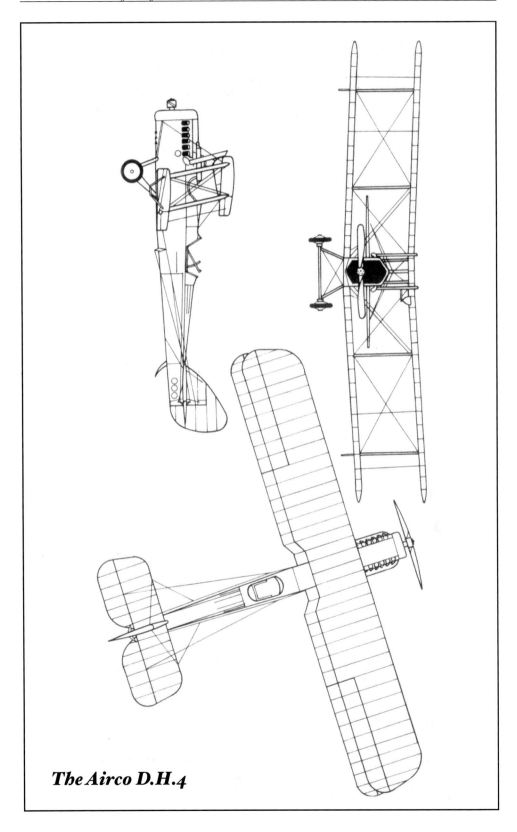

The Airco D.H.4

CHAPTER SIX

The Curtiss 'Jenny', Maid of all Work

In early 1914, even before the Great War had commenced, Curtiss had launched a programme to obtain Army contracts for its aircraft, and had managed to attract an English aircraft designer named B. Douglas-Thomas. This designer had worked with A.V..Roe and later transferred to the Sopwith Company. Having acquired valuable experience with these two companies in the design and construction of tractor aeroplanes, he agreed to design a similar type for Curtiss and immediately started work while still domiciled in England.

A few months later he moved across the Atlantic to the Hammondsport Curtiss plant to complete the project. Curtiss was impressed with the result and evidence of the aeroplane's origins could be seen in the fin and rudder shape and overall configuration. Although it resembled the de Havilland D.H.4, that appear two years later, thenew aircraft was conceived from his intimate knowledge of the tractor design.

However, the Curtiss Model J, as it came to be known, was at that time a thoroughly modern biplane powered by the well tried Curtiss OX 90-hp engine. It seated two in a canvas covered fuselage with all controls in the rear

The Curtiss Model "J" in completed form. The inital flight was made without fabric on the fuselage.

cockpit. The landing gear comprised twin wheels with a long skid in between, which was standard practice for those days. It could also be fitted with a central float and wing tip stabilisers.

The Model J took to the air for its maiden flight during the still, chill, days of early spring 1914 but records do not reveal whether it was in the wheel or float configuration. Logically the wheeled undercarriage arrangement would have been used as to convert the aircraft for water operation, which consisted removing the wheels and inserting a flat sided pontoon (a single large float) between the undercarriage skids, was a major modification. Under each wing tip a narrow vertical float with trailing ski acted as water stabilisers.

Curtiss delivered the company specification to the Chief of the Army Aviation Section, together with a factory price per unit based upon a given number. The specification, design and costs were accepted and an Army Contract (Order 653) of April 30, 1914, was given for a trainer for the Signal

Note the single star insignia on this JN4's fin/rudder. Mexico.

Corps. The controls incorporated the Curtiss shoulder yoke. This cumbersome method of control fitted around the shoulders of the pilot, responding to his natural movements. Left and right, forward and backwards with the aircraft following such movements for direction.

The modest success of the Model J led to the second Jenny ancestor, the Model N, submitted as an entry to the Army Competition of October 1914 for a reconnaissance aircraft. The event was cancelled as none of the competitors submitted a design that could safely meet the qualifying tests.

The Curtiss Model N.

The American Secretary of War approved a request by the Army for funds to develop a dedicated reconnaissance aircraft, and on July 1, 1914, the Signal Corps announced a competition to be held during the following October for the design and development of a standard service aircraft of advanced performance. The Specification stated is should have a maximum speed of 70 mph (minimum 40), fuel for four hours endurance at the top speed and carry a load of 450 pounds. Climb was set at 4000 feet in ten minutes. Range and climb requirements had to be met if any design was to compete.

A total of 30 companies were invited to tender and twelve accepted. This total was to be reduced to eight by October 7, as the Specification was considered too difficult. On October 20, just six entries were left and of these four had completed a prototype. Of this quartet only the Curtiss and Martin

Jenny waits for propeller to be swung at Post Field, 1918.

companies had built prototypes capable of complying with the Specification. Between October 23 and November 3, 1914, Martin and Curtiss took part in the trials. The Curtiss machine had its wings rigged to meet the stability requirement and did not attempt the endurance flight, but despite this, and other failures, the Cutiss N was declared the winner, if only because of the maximum speed of 82 mph and 40 during landing.

Curtiss Model JN/JN-2 'Jenny'.

Acceptance of the Curtiss trainer into the Army Aviation Section was due entirely to the efforts of Captain Cowan, the Commanding Officer at San Diego, as it was he who recommended that funds be allocated for the purchase of additional Model J trainers. This would cover the purchase of eight aeroplanes and four spare engines.

As a result the C.O. of the Aviation Section was to write to Curtiss on

December 14, requesting a quote for the supply of eight Model J Tractors 'to be modified as per Specification'. In its reply Curtiss queried the choice of engine, a 90-hp OX, and suggested the 100-hp OXX was more suitable due to its power rating. Agreement was reached and the quote altered to specify the use of 90 to 100-hp engines

All eight machines were completed by April 29, 1915, designated as the JN-2, and delivered to the First Aero Squadron (the first U.S. designed trainer to equip a total squadron) by June. Unfortunately the JN-2 was found to be wanting in many areas such as poor climb characteristics and control difficulties. At high speed it became unstable laterally. New engines and propellers were installed and a number of aircraft re-rigged. Eventually a damning report concluded by stating the JN-1 was unsuitable for military purposes. It was a blow to Curtiss who had been confident of being one of the chosen suppliers of aircraft to the Aviation Division.

The Canadian J-4 intrduced early in 1917, was developed from the JN-3 quite independently of the American production series. This was the first aeroplane in Canada to use skiis.

Curtiss JN-3.

The history of the JN-3 is rather obscure and was the direct result of the Army Signal Corps refusing the accept the JN-2 for service. It was this model that was eventually converted to become the JN-3, of which two were ordered in August 1915 by the Army Aviation Section. In the early months of the war Curtiss had, fortuitously, established a factory in Toronto, Canada, which was intended for the training of recruits wanting to be accepted as pilots for the R.F.C. (the British Royal Flying Corps).

The British Government Purchasing Commission wanted to buy the JN trainers and the opportunity of buying direct from the Curtiss Canadian factory

The Curtiss Jenny was used by the Americans during the U.S-Mexican war.

was ideal as both Canada, and England, could obtain supplies without America diverting aircraft for their own requirements. The Jenny, therefore, was placed in production as the intended trainer for British forces. Six were delivered to England in March 1915, and the Royal Naval Air Service took delivery of 97 some months later. As stated, the U.S.Army Signal Corps ordered two examples of the British model and they differed in many respects from the JN-2.

Lt G Carleton and his Jenny pictured during the Mexican war

Curtiss had, in the meantime, taken steps to improve the JN-2 and a factory engineer had arrived with replacement parts to start work on the suspect aircraft. Serial numbers 41 and 44 were the first to be converted to JN-3

JN-4D with clear-doped wings and star-in-circle markings that were adopted in May 1917.

standards, leaving 42, 43, 45 and 48 to follow. Serials 42, 45 and 48 were modified to accept JN-3 wings, and later the 100-hp OXX engine was installed.

Whatever the shortcomings, and criticisms, of the JN-2 the Army had little choice but to operate them during the American-Mexican War of 1916. They served with the First Aero Squadron attached to General Pershing's Army, and serials 42 to 45, 52 and 53, can be identified as serving.

JN4s undergoing repair and maintenance at Kelly Field, Texas, 1918.

Curtiss N-8 Model 1D.

It was the fiasco of the JN-2's performance in the U.S-Mexican war that led, indirectly, to the Model N-8. In March 1916 even before funds had been made available, the Signal Corps ordered eight aircraft, including four N-8s based upon a Specification issued by the Corps. Curtiss was instructed to deliver four JN-4 biplane tractors with increased wing area of 80 sq.ft. inserted into the upper wing centre section, and with 90-hp OX-2 engines. The wing modification resulted in a three bay design and, as the aeroplanes were completed, they had to be despatched to Columbus, New Mexico.

The N-8 was basically a JN-4B with the Curtiss 100-hp. OXX engine with a wider span centre-wing section, lower wing extensions and a central float plus

JN-4D on its nose, showing to advantage th 1918 markings, khaki-brown metal cowling, clear-doped fabric, and a comparision od upper and lower wingtip shapes

wing tip stabilisers. Also, the fin was taller. The U.S. Army ordered 14 but it was the Navy that was the principal user with a total of 560 as primary trainers.

The Curtiss JN-4 `Jenny'.

There were doubts in Army circles about the future use of the Curtiss trainers and reconnaissance biplanes as they had not performed well in the field. However, in England the story was different as the JN-3s had been accepted for use as primary trainers. The U.S. Signal Corps was still requiring the aeroplanes when America went to war in April 1917.

N-9, essentially a JN-4B with longer wings, was the standard U.S. Navy seaplane trainer od 1917-18 and the early post-war years. Note unique vertical radiattor design.

The U.S. Army ordered 800 bringing the total to 1500, of which the last ordered were not designated until later in the programme. First production aircraft were ordered during June 1917, 150 without engines, and it was not until January 1918 that deliveries commenced. Model 4As reached the training schools in July 1917.

There were a number of specially modified JN-4As such as number 1555 with a Curtiss OXX-6 of 100-hp flown at McCook Field in early 1918. Two other airframes were prototypes for the JN-4D with Hall-Scott engines. One 4A was fitted with a machin-gun synchroniser and used for trials as a fuselage only.

Curtiss Model JN-4B.

On August 1, 1916, the Signal Corps issued Specification No.1000 for a Primary Trainer, together with Specification 1001 for an Advanced Trainer. Three additional JN-4s were ordered to 1001 on August 29 for delivery by October 11. This second contract called for rapid production and the aircraft, together with spare OX-2 engines, were delivered between September/October.

Curtiss JN-4C.

Once again there was some confusion over the JN-4C Advanced Trainer of 1917, with that of the Canadian built version JN-4Can. However, production records reveal that only two genuine JN-4Cs were ever built, while some 1200-plus models of the `Canuck' were delivered.

In June 1918 an official of the Curtiss Company confirmed that the Signal Corps had directed the company to modify the Model 4B using the R.A.F Model 6 aerofoil in place of the standard Eiffel 36. Two machines were ordered

Curtiss JN4 'Jenny' stationed at Camp Borden, Canada.

on February 15, 1917, both to have Curtiss OXX-3 duel ignition engines. They carried U.S. serial 471/472 and were delivered to the U.S. Army in June 1917 along with two spare OXX-3s.

The new variant was an improvement over the 4B Series and quantity production was considered. However, by that time, after testing, the much improved JN-4D was in mass production and the 4C declared obsolete.

Prototype JN-4D had ailerons on both wings as the JN-4A and introduced the centre-section cutouts that were a feature of all subsequent JN models.

Curtiss Model JN-4D/4D-2.

The JN-4D variant was built in large numbers and was a modification of the JN-4A incorporating a number of the Canadian modifications. The Canadian Model JN-4D was the major production variant and used by all Allied Air

Rear cockpit of the JN-4D. Full compliment of insruments includes water temperature gauge, altimter, oil pressure gauge, and tachometer.

Forces. Following upon a May 3, 1917, meeting between the American and R.F.C officials Curtiss was directed to devote all it efforts to bring the JN-4 Series to production status.

On June 1 another, more significant, meeting took place between Curtiss, Daytown-Wright and U.S. Army officials. All were impressed by the Canadian-built JN-4 Canuck with its simplified control system, employing a joystick, ailerons on all four wing and other modifications. It was adjudged to be a superior design to all other previous JN Models.

Curtiss agreed to build a single prototype called the JN-4D (Model 1C) and completed it in four weeks. The engine had down-thrust settings and the exhaust stacks discharged above the upper wing. Ailerons were fitted on all wings. It resembled the standard Model 4A but under the skin it was a different aircraft.

To ensure that the supply of engines would be maintained the Aircraft Production Board decided upon the four-cylinder Hall-Scott Model A-7a in late May 1917. Two thousand were ordered as an initial batch, and Curtiss was requested to redesign the basic JN-4D to accept the modified unit. The subsequent aircraft supplied by Curtiss would be designated as HN-S4.

JN-4Ds with special colouring and markings of an Army Ambulance plane. Section behind rear cockpit lifts off to permit insertion of patient on a stretcher.

A number of Hall-Scott prototypes were built and delivered to McCook Field for testing, and series production was to be undertaken by the Fisher Body Corporation of Detroit. This company was the body manufacturing division of the General Motors Corporation. An order for 500 was placed on June 21, 1917, with the serial range 557 to 1056, and a second order was placed with the Daytown-Wright Corporation for a similar number.

However, by the time the 'tooling-up' had been completed the war was nearing its end and no contracts granted, with the result that all production of the JN-4D, Hall-Scott engine version, was cancelled and the serials switched to the Standard J Trainer. One prototype was tested at McCook Field, the second

The single JN-5 was a JN-4H modified by the Army to serve as a prototype for the JN-6.

at Fairchild, Ohio.

Assembly was started once again, but in the meantime Daytown Wright could not obtain the Hall-Scott engine. Curtiss asked to be relieved of the contract and this was agreed on September 19. In the following November the decision was taken to send the incomplete prototype to McCook Field. Both Dayton Wright and Fisher Body had also been asked to prepare drawings and modify a JN-4A aircraft. Fisher completed their order in January and it was delivered to McCook Field in February, designated as the JN-4D Special.

The **Model 4D-2** was a redesign by Curtiss in an attempt to introduce standardisation for the various sub-contractors. Often modifications were not introduced and many unauthorised modifications incorporated. In the summer of 1918 Curtiss were instructed by the Army to introduce the standardisation as the JN-4D-2, the suffix identifying the design of the second variant.

Work started on a prototype in August 1918 by the Bureau of Aircraft Production for delivery to Wright Field on September 25 for evaluation. Curtiss were hard pushed to complete detail drawings, and the St Louis Liberty Iron and Howell & Lesser companies, were given orders to undertake the engineering. By November all production drawings had been completed but the Armistice was just days away and all contracts cancelled. The Army still wanted to test the prototype under a separate contract, and it was delivered to McCook Field and designated as the P-100.

Although the Army operated just one 4D-2, a total of 4074 JN-4s were delivered and Curtiss built a number of civil versions. However, this market was not interested in purchasing a new JN-4D-2 when any number of surplus aircraft were selling at $3000 or less by the Army.

Curtiss Model 1E, JN-4H.

JN-4H airframe was identical to the JN-4D except for revised nose contours and radiator shape necessary to accommodate the 150 Wright-Hispano engine.

Curtiss had been examining the Hispano-Suiza Model A engine of 150-hp that was scheduled for use in the S.E.5 production fighter, the first of which had been delivered to the Army by Wright-Martin in November. It was arranged for one engine to be delivered to Curtiss and the company speedily modified a JN-4 airframe in eight days and, during its flight, it had reached a maximum speed of 95.5 mph.

The designation of JN-4H was applied, indicating that it was powered by the Hispano-Suiza engine. By November 26 an order was placed by the Signal Corps for 600 examples and, during the following month, it was awarded priority. The order, No.20431, was received on January 5, 1918 in the serial range 37933 to 38532, 400 of which were to be called the JN-4HT, the T suffix indicating its use as a Trainer. The other 600 became the JN-4HG gunnery instruction version, and the JN-4HB Bomber Trainer. Two additional HT and HG airframes were ordered.

The American Navy demanded its quota of the Hisso Jennies, and while

Curtiss JN-4D refuelling at Post Field, 1916.

priority was given to Army orders is was decided a number should go to the Senior Service. The Navy, every week, required five of the Model 4HT. The Navy needed the Jenny as the Allies were losing too many surface ships to the German U-boat.

Thirty JN-4Hs were delivered in March 1918 with the serials A3205 to 3234. The Navy also had three JN-4Ds and seven others. A further 90 NHs were asked for by the Navy from Army stocks to train air gunners, plus 56 JN-4HG two gun trainers.

The JN-4H was also chosen as the preferred vehicle for carriage of the U.S. Mail

Student pilot stand by the wreckage of his JN-4H Jenny.

from Washington to New York. Six 4Hs were delivered and after modification were also known as the JN-4HM.

The JN-6H was a development of the 4H with ailerons on all wings, a balanced rudder and swept upper wing. These and other changes resulted in the change of designation. A total of 150 were ordered as JH-6B Bomber Trainers, 100 6HO Observation and 125 Pursuit HP. The HG became the 6HG-1 with the Marlin machine-guns as armament, and the 6HG-2 with the Marlin and Lewis guns. Later the new Colt Browning .303 in. gun was considered but never installed.

A total of 560 HG-1s were ordered on August 6, 1918, but Curtiss was again inundated with orders for several variants, and in the event only 480 were delivered, a number of which had the more powerful Hispano-Suiza engine of 180-hp.

Curtiss Model 1F JN-6 Series.

With the large numbers of the JN-4 in service faults in performance and associated areas were thrown up. The Army held negotiations with Curtiss in May 1918 to assess the amount of disruption that would arise on the production lines of the main supplier and sub-contractors plants. The consensus was that the modifications were so numerous it would be more practical to incorporate them in a new variant.

The decision came in May with the new variant having ailerons on all wings, a balanced rudder, additional fin bracing, the control stick installed as standard and moving the upper wing aft by 7.7 in. Curtiss produced the drawings, which were immediately approved, and the design was called the JN-6H.

The initial order to Curtiss was for 600 examples fitted with the Hispano-Suiza

RFC student pilots in formation for the camera, Texas, USA

engines, with a second for 700 which would incorporate any additional modifications as they were required. The first order was divided into the variations of the main design with 150 bomber JN-6HB bombers; 100 JN-6HO observation trainers equipped with a Type L semi-automatic plate camera, and 125 JN-6HP pursuit trainers. The HPs also had a camera gun to assess the number of strikes. On 18 June 1918 the Army placed orders for 90 JN-HG2, two gun trainers, to be followed by a second order of 6 August for 560 JN-6HG-1 single gun trainers. The total on order in October 1918 was 1035 JN-6Hs.

The 6HG gunnery trainers were soon to be modified to accept the new Model 1 Hisso engine and Browning .303 in. machine-gun. Also, the new Marlin MG8 .30 in. gun was specified. Deliveries started in September 1918 but lacked the Browning armament. An order for six 'Special Duty' 6Hs was placed in October and delivered in March 1919. The more powerful Hispano-Suiza Model E of 180-hp was ready but none installed in the Jenny Series.

Discussions were held in March 1918, just as the American Army was ready to move to France, and the decision was taken to switch priority of aircraft deliveries to the Navy in the Atlantic and North Sea. The first delivery of crew trainers was the DH-4 and the Curtiss JN-4Ts, approximately 40 reached the Navy.

The following May the Navy asked for more trainers and 56 JN-4HG two-gun trainers for bomber gunner training. Delivery of the final variants of the

JN-6HG-1s took place in October. The Navy was also supplied with 6HG-1s for the Marines, who were involved in an expedition to Dominica.

Curtiss JN-5H.

Despite huge deliveries of Jenny trainers to the Signal Corps and England, it was regarded by the Army as being no better than other types available. In February McCook Field was finalising plans for a competition to be held the following month to find a Jenny replacement. The Army was operating a number of JN-4As, but the main variant was the 4D. Curtiss was instructed to modify the Hispano-Suiza powered 4H to compete with the other competitive designs.

Curtiss had only days to provide any suitable conversion and chose to modify the 4H as the JN-5H. It was an almost impossible situation for Curtiss, but the challenge was accepted and the altered Jenny's main modification was a reduced wing span. To save time a set of new wings were despatched to McCook Field for installation of a standard 4H. McCook engineers rejected this rushed compromise modification, which left Curtiss with no choice but to offer a new design fuselage with the engine moved aft, increased fuel capacity, a smaller tailplane and balanced rudder. The wing dihedral was omitted.

The Army approved the prototype if only to have a Curtiss competition entry and applied the designation of JN-5H. It was delivered to McCook on March 18, 1918, having flown for the first time four days earlier, and with two

Late production Canadian JN-4 with 1918 U.S. military markings.

sets of wings, original and new. First trials with the original set took place with the competition starting on March 20 and continuing for five days. It was a forgone conclusion that the superior Vought VE-7 would be the successful entry. However, the Curtiss 5H remained at McCook for further trials with the Hisso Model E engine of 180-hph and a new set of metal framed wings.

Cutiss Model R2 and R4.

Design and development of the Model 2 R-Series of biplanes was started after the first J-Series had been constructed and tested as a more advanced variant of the J and N powered by the new Curtiss VX engine of 160-hp, The company specification called it a `Fast Scout'.

By August 1915 the `R' prototype had been modified in many ways with the upper wing moved aft, the long two-seat cockpits forward, a fixed fin/rudder and a modified undercarriage. Engine and propeller failures were a constant problem and a lot of effort was made to cure the faults which were finally traced to propeller flutter. Curtis also provided a smaller diameter, four and two-blade metal units. For armament trials a number of Lewis guns were installed on a Scarff ring in the rear cockpit.

The **Model R-2A** prototype was completed before the prototype R with minor modifications, while the **R-3** was a naval version and fitted with twin floats and wider span (57 ft 1 in.) wings by increasing the area of the centre section and additional wing panels. The Army ordered eighteen R-3s in 1916 with delivery scheduled for 1917. However, it appears that they may have been improved and re-built as R-6s or R-9s.

Curtiss R-4

The R-4 was an improved model of the R-2 with the more powerful Curtiss V-2-3 200-hp engines, fifteen of which were to have single controls in the rear cockpit. Controls were either a Curtiss yoke, which was cumbersome, or the more practical single column joystick. Just one, the final production aircraft, had dual control. Thirty-six R-4s were ordered the same month as the first contract, together with 24 spare engines. One aeroplane was used for reconnaissance and fitted with a camera, while a second was flight tested for bombing duties.

The **R-4L** of which twelve were delivered to the Army were, primarily, engine test beds, in particular for the new, 12 cylinder Liberty. Such was the improved performance figures of these trial ships that a number of R-4s were modified to accept the new engine and their designation changed to R-4L.

The **R-4LM.** When the Army was delegated to initiate a mail service in May 1918, it was decided to use the R-4L variant. This mail service was re-assigned to the Post Office in August that year and, when they planned to extend the service, they requested delivery of six more R-4Ls. But, the Army had none and a new modification of the R-Series was commenced.

Curtiss Model R-6

Twin JN used JN-4 wing panels and engines on a modified fuselage. Starboard engine modified to turn opposite to port engine to neutralise propeller torque in flight.

The **R-6** was the wider wing-span version of the R-3, with its 200-hp Curtiss V-2-3 engine. A grand total of 76 were delivered to the Navy and fitted with twin floats, except for one with a single, central float. The floats could be removed for wheels to be installed and a number were delivered to France in January 1918. The Army made enquiries and this led to an order for eighteen, but they were eventually re-directed to the Navy.

The **R-6L** was the R-6 modification and was in fact forty Navy conversions. They were powered by the low-compression 360-hp Liberty engine and used for a torpedo/bombing role. Fourteen further conversions were modified from R-9s.

Curtiss Model R-7.

One aeroplane with 200-hp Curtiss engine purchased by the New York Times. There is no confirmation of this designation.

Curtiss Model R-9. The bomber version of the R-6 with pilot in the front cockpit and bombardier in rear. Ten were transferred from the Navy to the Army in February 1918. An interesting experiment by Curtiss was an attempt to produce a pusher version of the R-Series using the Model R wings, cockpit pod with the pusher engine installed in the rear section.

Curtiss Model 1B Twin JN.

In addition to developing military aeroplanes for the U.S. Army and Navy, the Curtiss design department was occupied with development of a number of Private Venture (PV), one of which was development of the Jenny.

Work started in 1916 when the company sponsored a larger, twin-engine

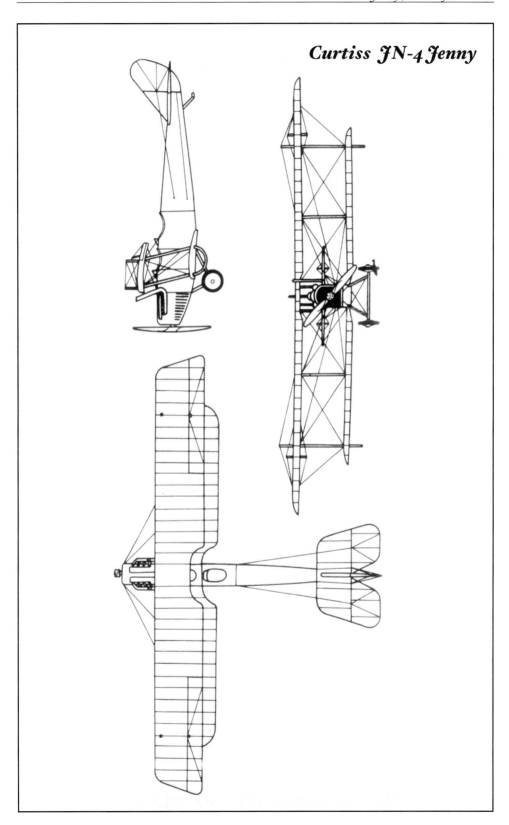

Curtiss JN-4 Jenny

version of the J-Series. To speed production of a prototype the company decided to make use of major assemblies of the, then, new JN-4 Series. As a result two sets of outer wing panels were assembled to a re-designed centre-section of 11 ft. 4 in. width.

The prototype made its first flight in April 1916 and established several record breaking long distance flights. The Aero Club of America agreed to launch a campaign to purchase the new aeroplane for the nation, and a number of other associations agreed to contribute funds.

The U.S. Army, after much persuasion, agreed to purchase an example that was different from early prototypes in having the undercarriage struts located under the engines, plus larger main wheels and a nose wheel. The Army also requested a formal quotation for six aircraft, five spare engines and other spares. The designation of JN-5 for the Army was applied, but the design was always known as the Twin JN.

Work started on the order without the benefit of a formal contract and one was delivered to the Army with a wheeled undercarriage, plus two for the Navy, which had twin floats. It was not until October 13, 1916, that the order was finally placed and it included eight spare OXX-2 engines. The contract demanded many modifications and all were delivered during October and November 1916.

CHAPTER SEVEN

de Havilland D.H.1 and D.H.2

Airco, the Aircraft Manufacturing Company, was established by G.Holt Thomas early in 1912 and held the British rights for the manufacture of the French Farman aeroplanes. For some time the company had been content with this arrangement but, for some time, Holt Thomas had wanted to establish a design department of his own, and in June 1914 he secured the services of Geoffrey de Havilland.

Mr de Havilland (later to be knighted) came into the Aircraft Manufacturing Co., with a wealth of experience of aircraft design and construction. Not only had he designed and flown the Royal Aircraft Factory's most successful types during his period of service there, but he had also seen many examples of other manufacturers products that had gone to Farnborough to be tested. For the Aircraft Manufacturing Co., he designed a series of remarkably good aeroplanes, several of which made substantial contributions towards the attainment of supremacy in the air for the Allies. These aircraft earned for their designer the unique compliment of being known by his name rather than that of the manufacturer. 'Airco' seldom prefaced the numerical D.H. designations.

The D.H.1 was not Geoffrey de Havilland's first design by any means but it was the first aeroplane designed by him for the Aircraft Manufacturing Co. It was intended for reconnaissance and fighting duties, and the lack of a machine-gun interrupter gear inevitably made it into a two-seat 'pusher' biplane. 'Pusher' described the action of the propeller to power the aircraft. With the engine fitted behind the pilot and facing towards the rear it 'pushed' the aircraft forward. The forward cockpit was occupied by the Observer/Gunner who thus had a clear view to fire a machine-gun without the fear of being obstructed by the propeller. The D.H.1 was powered by a 70-hp Renault engine and appeared in January 1915. The wings were of two bay construction and the tail unit was supported on the customary booms. The undercarriage on the prototype incorporated coil springs and concealed oleo struts, and when it first appeared the D.H.1 was fitted with air brakes. These consisted of two small aerofoils, each of about three feet span disposed on either side of the nacelle and pivoted on an axis that crossed the fuselage just behind the forward centre section struts. They could be rotated through 90 degrees to present a flat surface to the

One of the first production batch of Airco/D.H.1.

D.H.1A prototype

airstream. The air brakes were not successful, however, and were soon abandoned

The test flights were made by Geoffrey de Havilland, and the D.H.1 had quite a good performance despite the fact that it had been designed for a more powerful engine. The intention was to fit the 120-hp Beardmore as the standard power unit. But the Royal Aircraft Factory had laid claim to the few Beardmore engines that were available in 1914 and production of the D.H design was

D.H.1 stands outside the company's hangar. No gun installation.

inevitably delayed. Some, however, were built with the Renault engine and these differed from the prototype in having exhaust manifolds that led the gases well forward, presumably to avoid damage to the airscrew. In the production machines the forward cockpit was cut much lower than on the prototype in order to facilitate the use of a gun, and the undercarriage relied upon the more usual rubber chord for shock absorbers.

When eventually powered by the Beardmore engine the aircraft was re-designated D.H.1A and was identical in appearance to the production D.H.1 apart from the bulkier upright engine behind the pilot's cockpit

By the time production could be undertaken, the Aircraft Manufacturing Co., were too busy with later designs, and the D.H.1A was built by Savages of King's Lynn under sub-contract. The type never achieved any prominence with comparatively few being built, and only six went overseas. These went to the relative obscurity of the Middle East, the others were distributed to Home Defence and training units. However, the D.H.1 design is of historic interest, not only as the first of the long line of distinguished D.H. types which was continued after the demise of the Aircraft Manufacturing Co., but also as the immediate predecessor of the more famous D.H.2

D.H.1 & D.H.1a Specifications

Dimensions

Wing Span:	41 ft	
Chord:	5 ft 6 in.	
Gap:	5 ft 7 in.	
Dihedral:	3 degrees.	
Incidence:	D.H.1	4 degrees 30'.
	D.H.1A	5 degrees 15'.
Span of tail:	D.H.1	12 ft 6 in.
	D.H.1A	12 ft 3 in.
Length:	D.H.1	29 ft 0 in.
	D.H.1A	28 ft 11 in.
Height:	D.H.1	11 ft 4 in.
	D.H.1A	11 ft 2 in.

Areas.

Wings upper:	187 sq. ft	
lower:	175 sq. ft	
Total:	362 sq. ft	
Ailerons each:	16 sq. ft	
Total:	64 sq. ft	
Tailplane:	37.5 sq. ft	
Elevators:	23 sq. ft.	
Rudder:	15.5 sq. ft	
Wheel track	5 ft 10 in.	
Airscrew diameter:	D.H.1	9 ft 0 in.
	D.H.1A	8 ft 10 in.
Weights:	D.H.1	Empty 1356 lbs.
		Loaded 2044 lbs.
	D.H.1A	Empty 1610 lbs.
		Loaded 2340 lbs.
Power.	D.H.1.	170-hp Renault.
	D.H.1A	120-hp Beardmore.

Performance: D.H.1 Maximum speed at 3500 ft 80 mph. Climb to 3500 ft 11 min.15 sec. D.H.1A. Maximum speed at ground level 90 mph, at 2000 ft 89 mph, at 4000 ft 88 mph, at 6000 ft 90 mph, at 8000 ft 90 mph, at 10,000 ft 86 mph, at 12,000 ft 84 mph. Climb to 1000 ft 1 min. 40 sec, to 2000 ft 3 min. 35sec, to 3000 ft 3 min. 55 sec, to 3500 ft 6 min. 27 sec, to 4000 ft 8 min.15 sec, to 5000 ft 10 min. 25 sec, to 6000 ft 13 min 10 sec, to 7000 ft 16 min. 20sec, to 8000ft 19 min. 30 sec. to 9000 ft 23 min, to 10,000 ft 27.min. 30 sec. to 11,000 ft 32 min. 25 sec, to 12,000 ft 38 min. 25 sec. Service ceiling 13,500 ft.

Tankage: D.H.1, petrol 50 gallons. D.H.1A main pressure tank 35.3 gallons, service gravity tank 5.5 gallons, total 40.8 gallons. Oil 23. gallons. Water 5 gallons.

Armament: One Lewis machine gun on pillar mounting in front cockpit.

Manufacturer: Aircraft Manufacturing Co., Ltd.,Hendon, London N.W.

Other contractor: Savages Ltd, Kings Lynn, Norfolk.

D.H.1A of No. 14 Squadron.

Service use. There were no units completely equipped with the D.H.1s or 1As. The type was issued to some Home Defence and training units, including No. 35 Reserve Squadron, Northolt. Six went to the Middle East Brigade in 1916 where some were used operationally by No. 14 Squadron, R.F.C.

Production and allocation. The total number of D .H.1s and 1As delivered to the R.F.C. was 73. Of that total 43 went to training units, 24 to Home Defence units and six to the Middle East Brigade.

Serial numbers. 4606, 4607, A.1611 - A.1660.

Costs. Airframe without engine, instruments and gun £1,100.

70-hp Renault engine £523.10s   120-hp Beardmore engine £825.0s

de Havilland D.H.2

The second de Havilland design to be built by the Aircraft Manufacturing Co., was a small single-seat, fighting scout in which the designer's first concern had been to give the pilot effective forward-firing armament. It was, therefore, decided that the 'pusher' design should be retained with the result that the D.H.2 looked very much like a scaled-down D.H.1 .

Some histories seen to imply that the D.H.2 was deliberately designed and produced as a counter-weapon to the Fokker Monoplane, which, with its synchronised machine-gun, wrought great havoc among the Allied two-seaters in late 1915 and early 1916. In point of fact, the design of the D.H.2 was neither

A D.H.2 of the second production batch.

demanded nor prompted by the Fokker menace any more than was that of its companion Fokker-beater, the Royal Aircraft Factory F.E.2b; it simply so happened that these aeroplanes proved to be effective counter-weapons. The prototype D.H.2 completed its flight trials in July, 1915, at the time when the Fokker Monoplane was only beginning to be encountered; the first contract for quantity production was awarded during the following month, and the first production machine arrived in France in December, 1915 When the D.H.2 was designed, the technique of using a fixed-gun and aiming the whole aeroplane at the target was not at first accepted by Britain, although it had been successfully demonstrated by French pilots. The prototype D.H.2 therefore, did not have a fixed machine-gun, nor even a central mounting for a semi-free weapon. Instead, a movable bracket was fitted on each side of the cockpit in line with the windscreen, and from these the pilot was expected to aim his Lewis gun while flying his aircraft in the manoeuvres of combat. As a result, the nacelle of the prototype had a rather different appearance from that of the production D.H.2 For a pusher, the D.H.2 was remarkably neat and compact, and was of great structural strength. It was a two-bay biplane, and the tail-booms formed a 'V' in plan; the tail-unit was obviously inherited from the D.H.1. The undercarriage was of the 'vee' type, and the steerable tailskid was mounted on an extension of the rudder post. The standard engine was the 100-hp Gnôme Monosoupape rotary, but a version also existed with the 110-hp Le Rhône.

The first R.F.C. squadron to be completely equipped with the D.H.2 was No.

The mangled wreck of D.H.2, 5994, of No. 29 Squadron shot down on August 25, 1918. Pilot Lt K K Turner

24, which was commanded by Major Lanoe George Hawker, V.C. This unit had been formed at Hounslow on September 1, 1915, and received its D.H.2s at the end of the year. No. 24 Squadron had the distinction of being the first single-seat fighter squadron to go to any battlefront when it flew its twelve D.H.2s from Hounslow to St Omer on February 7, 1916. Two other D.H.2 squadrons followed; No. 29 on March 25, and No. 32 on May 28, 1916.

Lieutenant Tidmarsh opened the scoring for No. 24 Squadron on April 2, 1916, when he shot down an enemy machine near Bapaume; and from that date

D.H.2, No. 6011, of 24 Squadron brought down by a member of Kampfgeschwader *1.*

onwards 'Hawker's Squadron' did much successful fighting.

Although the D.H.2 eventually proved to be more pleasant to fly than any other contemporary pusher scout, operational or experimental, it was not at first popular with the pilots. It was extremely sensitive on the controls, a characteristic of great value in combat but, in an aeroplane with a small speed range, likely to cause the machine to spin easily. Until the D.H.2 pilots began to understand their mounts several casualties were cause by spinning as this phenomenon was not, at that time, understood. In one such accident the D.H.2 had caught fire while spinning and the aircraft was, thereafter, known by the unjustly grim sobriquet the 'Spinning Incinerator'. Second Lieutenant S.E.Cowan, M.C., of No. 24 Squadron did much to inspire the confidence of pilots in the aircraft by his skilful handling of his D.H.2, and he was the first pilot to perform stunts. It soon was appreciated that the D.H.2 was capable of executing all normal aerobatics

Other dangers were endemic, however, to the flying of rotary powered pushers and the historian of No. 24 Squadron recorded:

> Two splendid pilots, Lieutenant Glew and Captain Wilson, were killed by cylinders blowing out and severing the tail booms of their machine. Several other pilots, notably Captain Hughes Chamberlain and Lieutenant Sibley, had the narrowest of escapes.

The gun mounting on production machines still had a certain amount of flexibility, but pilots soon adopted the technique of aiming the whole aeroplane at the target and, thereafter, the gun's flexibility was seldom used in combat.

A captured D.H.2 being inspected by German ground troops.

That the D.H.2 proved its worth soon after the arrival of the squadrons in France is borne out in the report written of May 23, 1916, by Sir Henry Rawlinson, General Officer commanding the Fourth Army.

> ... and the de Havilland machine has unquestionably proved itself superior to the Fokker in speed, manoeuvre, climbing and general efficiency.

This aircraft is the subject of the colour artwork in the plate section.

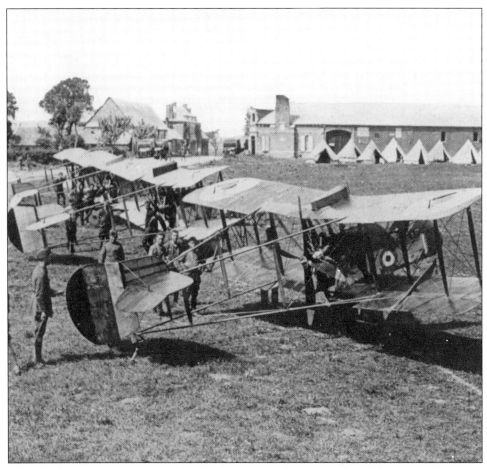

D.H.2s of No. 32 Squadron, R.F.C., at Vert Galant, Ferme, circa June 1916.

The D.H.2 showed its mettle in many combats during the Battle of the Somme and on into 1917 but never better than on the evening of July 20, 1916. Four aircraft of No. 24 Squadron's machines, led by Captain R.E.A.W. Hughes-Chamberlain, fought eleven enemy aircraft over Flers and destroyed three of them.

One of the earliest outstanding individual combats against great odds was that fought on July 1, 1916, by Major L.W.B.Rees, the officer commanding No. 32 Squadron. Major Rees was flying a D.H.2 and was awarded a Victoria Cross for his action. From a distance he saw a formation of enemy bombers – the formation had just shot down and killed one of his own pilots, Second Lieutenant J.C.Simpson, who had gallantly and single-handedly attacked. As soon as Rees recognised the nationality of the bombers he attacked them, forced two down, broke up the enemy formation and caused them to abandon the raid. Although wounded in the thigh Major Rees fought until his ammunition was exhausted and only then did he break off the fight

Captain L.P.Aizlewood of No. 32 Squadron owed his life to the sturdy construction of the D.H.2. On September 9, 1916, he was flying one of three D.H.2s that had engaged five enemy machines over Thiepval. He dived on one of the German biplanes and closed to twenty yards before opening fire, but he

A D.H.2 with a four-blade airscrew that later became standard.

was so intent on his target that his D.H.2 struck the tail of the enemy machine. Aizlewood's propeller was smashed and his undercarriage wrecked. The tail booms were also badly damaged, yet he brought his D.H.2 down near the British lines without being injured. His opponent crashed near Miraumont.

No. 24 Squadron went far towards establishing a tradition of fighting against great odds. On September 15 three D.H.2s attacked seventeen enemy aircraft near Morval, they shot down two and scattered the remainder. Again on

Cockpit of a D.H.2 with a mounted machine-gun.

October 26 five D.H.2s of the squadron fought twenty enemy single-seat fighters near Bapaume. Most of the German machines were Halberstadts, faster than the D.H.2s and able to out-climb their British adversaries, but, unlike the German machines, the little pushers did not lose height when turning and so were able to outfight the enemy.

By this time, however, the D.H.2 had generally begun to be outclassed by the new Albatros and Halberstadt scouts. However, replacements did not begin until March 1917 and, during the winter of 1916-17, the type fought on gallantly but not without loss. But, before the D.H.2's star began to wane, it was indirectly responsible for the death of one of the early German fighting pilots of first rank.

On October 8, 1916, Oswald Boelcke, victor in forty aerial combats, led his flight of six Albatros D.Is to attack two D.H.2s of 'C' Flight, No. 24 Squadron. The British machines were flown by Lieutenant A.G.Knight and second Lieutenant A.E.McKay. Boelcke dived to attack Knight at the same time as one of his pilots, Erwin Bohme, selected the same D.H.2 as his objective. Bohme's undercarriage struck Boelcke's upper wing and the German leader dropped away from the fight. At first it appeared that his Albatros was under control, but the wings later broke away and Boelcke went down to his death.

One of the pilots of Boelcke's flight on that day was Manfred von Richthofen, who succeeded to the command of *Jagdstaffel* 2 and who, in less than one month, was to avenge his former leader's death by depriving No. 24 Squadron of their Commanding Officer. On November 23, 1916, the D.H.2 of Major Lanoe George Hawker, V.C., fell to Richthofen's guns after one of the longest individual air combat of the war.

Shortly after Hawker's death another British pilot, who was to prove a worthy successor, began his fighting career flying a D.H.2. This was Flight Sergeant (later Major) J.T.B.McCudden who was a member of No. 29 Squadron. From a combat on November 9, 1916, he brought his D.H.2 back with 24 bullet holes in it, a greater number than he was to sustain in any of his subsequent fights.

No. 20 was the first D.H.2 Squadron to be re-equipped when in March 1917 it exchanged its pushers for Nieuport Scouts. Squadron No. 24 and 32 were to have received the new D.H.5 but their re-equipment was not completed until June.

The D.H.2 was not supplied in quantity to Hone Defence squadrons, but in the early hours of the morning of June 17, 1917, Captain R.H.M.S Sandby attacked Zeppelin L.48 over Therberton. He was flying a D.H.2 from the Orfordness Experimental Station and attacked at the same moment as Lieutenant L.P.Watkins on No. 37 Squadron. Sandby was credited with destroying the enemy airship while Watkins delivered the *coup de grâce*.

A few D.H.2s were used in Palestine. No. 111 Squadron had three on its strength during October 1917, and a detachment from No. 24 Squadron, known as 'X' Flight and had begun its work with SPADs and three B.E.12s, received one D.H.2 also in October 1917. In Macedonia 'A' Flight of No. 47 Squadron received one D.H.2 in October 1917, long after they were outclassed even in that secondary theatre of war. Two of No. 47's D.H.2s were supplied to Lieutenant General G.F.Milne at the end of March 1917 as part of the R.F.C's contribution towards the creation of a composite fighter squadron. The rest of this mixed unit consisted of four of the R.F.C's B.E.12s, together with the R.N.A.S. contribution of four Sopwith 1 1/2 Strutters and a Sopwith Triplane.

Official statistics record that one D.H.2 was sent to the B.E.F in France in 1918 but by the autumn of that year none were left on charge with the R.A.F. The D.H.2 was essentially an aeroplane of the early period of the war in the air, but in its day it was nevertheless one of the most effective aerial weapons of the First World War.

D.H.2 Specifications

Dimensions.
Wing span: 28 ft 3 in. Length: 25 ft 23 in. Height: 9 ft 7 in Chord: 4 ft 9 in. Gap: 4 ft 9 in. Dihedral: 4 degrees. Incidence: 3 degrees. Span of tail: 10 ft 3 in. Wheel track: 5 ft 10 in. Airscrew diameter: Gnôme 8 ft 0 in. Le Rhône 8 ft 3 in.
Areas:
Wings upper: 128 sq. ft, lower: 121 sq. ft, total: 249 sq. ft. Ailerons each: 14 sq. ft. Total: 56 sq. ft. Tailplane: 20.6 sq. ft. Elevators: 13.5 sq. ft. Fin: 2.7 sq. ft. Rudder: 11 sq. ft.
Power: 100-hp Gnôme Monosoupape, 110-hp Le Rhône
Armament: One Lewis machine-gun on flexible mounting in front of pilot, normally fixed to fire forward. Drums of ammunition were carried in racks outside the cockpit.
Manufacturer: The Aircraft Manufacturing Co., Ltd, Hendon, London, N.W.

Service use.
Western Front; R.F.C. Squadrons Nos. 24, 29 and 32. Some D.H.2s on strength of Squadrons Nos. 5, 11 and 18. Palestine; No. 111 Squadron and 'X' Flight. Macedonia 'A' Flight of No. 47 Squadron. R.F.C. and R.N.A.S. Composite Fighting Squadron. Training, used at various training units,

including No.10 Reserve Squadron at Joyce Green.

Production and Allocation.
A total of 400 D.H.2s were delivered to the R.F.C. of which 266 went to the British Expeditionary Force (B.E.F.) in France. Thirty-two to the Middle East, two to Home Defence units and 100 to training units.

Serial numbers.
Between and about 5023 and 6008, 7842-7941 (renumbered ex-R.F.C., D.H.2 transferred to Admiralty as sample. A.2533 - A.2632, A.4764 - A.4813, A.4988 - A.5087.

Notes on Individual Machines.
Used by No. 24 Squadron A.2533 - A-2632, A.4664 -A.4813, A.4988-A.5087. 7918,7930. A.2541, A.2544, A.3563, A.2564, A.2581, A.2592. A.2606, A.5007, A.5018. Other machines, 5985, No. 29 Squadron. 7887 shot down September 1916. A.2599 and A.4798, both of No. 10 Reserve Squadron.

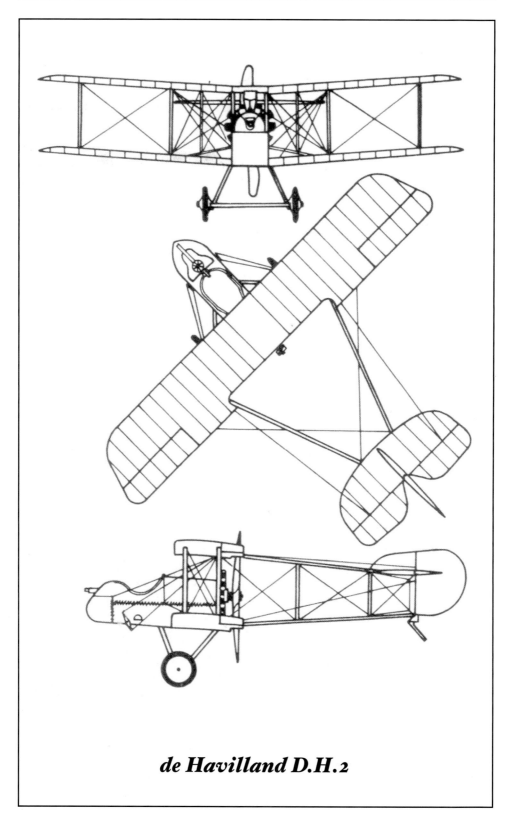

de Havilland D.H.2